2/15/13

J [barcode] D0857451

S. g... nected at

Did 2.0.

Have to say that our cab ride to the airport was one of the highlights of that trip.

Seriously enjoyed our interaction.

Thanks for joining us tonight for one of our Collective Bias Family Dinners.

It's All About Relationships!

TEd

In the connection economy, trust and relationships are the new currency. It's not a soft thing you do in your spare time, it's the heart and soul of your business.

—Seth Godin, Author of *Tribes*

In a wonderfully digestible form, *Return on Relationship* explains the paradigm shift present in the social media "conversation" and outlines the practical steps a marketer *can* and *must* take today.

—Dr. Tamara Monosoff, Social Entrepreneur, Best-selling Business Author and Trainer, Founder of TamaraMonosoff.com & MomInvented.com

This is a book where you can learn to cash in on social media. Ted Rubin and Kathryn Rose show you and every organization how to take it to the bank.

—Jeffrey Hayzlett, Global Business Celebrity, Bestselling Author, *Sometime Cowboy*

Return on Relationship is a powerful read and an important reminder to business people everywhere that it's people that matter most. In today's advertising-cluttered world, this book is a must-read to help you grow your business, one relationship at a time.

—Dave Kerpen, *New York Times* Bestselling Author of *Likeable Social Media* and *Likeable Business*

Ted Rubin and Kathryn Rose see eye to eye with me on this. A company that intends to survive in the modern business environment needs to master the art of building relationships of value. This isn't touchy-feely. This is pure business survival.

—Chris Brogan, CEO, Human Business Works, and co-author of *The Impact Equation*

This excellent, common-sense approach to applying the best principles of human relationships to modern brand marketing gives new salience to the idea that today business is indeed "social."

—Marisa Thalberg, Vice President, Corporate Global Digital Marketing, The Estée Lauder Companies, Inc. and Founder, ExecutiveMoms.com

Humanity has made a triumphant return to the marketplace! In *Return on Relationship*, Ted Rubin and Kathryn Rose help move us all forward by looking back to the basics of what it's all really about.

—Morgan Johnston, Manager Corporate Communication at JetBlue Airways

Ted and Kathryn's book will turn your corporate head around…toward the customer, with the right voice and approach to build *real* relationships through social media.

—Sam Decker Founder & CEO Mass Relevance

Ted Rubin and Kathryn Rose make the case that investing in relationships can turn social currency into tangible, financial returns. The guidelines in this book will prove valuable to marketers in the decade ahead and beyond, regardless of which social media channels and technologies are in vogue at any time. *Return on Relationship* strikes the right balance between marketers needing to take control over their brand while acknowledging the central role consumers play.

—David Berkowitz,
Vice President of Emerging Media, 360i

Return on Relationship is a unique reminder that people, not platforms, are what drive positive and meaningful engagement in our new digital world. Ted Rubin and Kathryn Rose remind us of the key questions we should be asking ourselves about what should be driving our engagement with clients, friends, and fans and how relationships are the most important part of anyone's job. This book will be on my "must-read" list for people I work with, serve, mentor, and admire. Anyone who values communication or has "communications" or "public relations" in their title should be paying attention and reading with a highlighter in hand!

—Aaron H. Sherinian, Vice President,
Communications and Public Relations,
United Nations Foundation

Ted Rubin and Kathryn Rose understand the new world of marketing because they live it every day. The new marketer must build real relationships with consumers, partners, suppliers, and clients. No technology can do this for you; it requires rolled-up sleeves, responsiveness, and getting to know someone beyond a Big Data profile. Ted and Kathryn are masters of this craft and they share ROR (#RonR) with us all.

—John Andrews, Founder/CEO Collective Bias

Ted and Kathryn understand that marketing at its core has always been about relationships. *Return on Relationship* will help your business win in this new hyper-connected era! I hope you are ready. Your customers are.

—Frank Eliason, Author of *@YourService*,
Global Director of Social Media, Citi

Ted and Kathryn hit it out of the park with their book *Return on Relationship*. Relationships are the new currency, and brands and individuals will benefit if they understand and value the power of personal connection.

—Porter Gale, Marketer and Author of
Your Network Is Your Net Worth,
Former CMO Virgin America

When it comes to success in social media, there is nothing more important for brands to understand than the value of relationships. Social media is about people stories, not product stories. Ted and Kathryn understand this and provide a unique and insightful perspective on how to drive results in social to help brands truly maximize their return on relationships.

—Avi Savar, Founder & CEO Big Fuel

In their new book *Return on Relationship*, Ted Rubin and Kathryn Rose explain the shift in mind-set needed to be a successful marketer in today's new social age. This book is a must-read for any marketer who sees the transformational force of social and wants prescriptive steps to navigate the new fundamentals.

—Tami Canizzaro,
IBM, Executive Director of Marketing

Ted Rubin and Kathryn Rose have got it right. Relationships matter much more than transactions. *Return on Relationship* is timely, compelling, and valuable. Highly recommended!

—Rob Fuggetta, Founder & CEO, Zuberance,
Author Brand Advocates

In *ROR*, Ted and Kathryn make you think about the 5th and 6th P of Marketing, People and Purpose. In the end, that's what relationships are about...not numbers.

—Brian Solis, Principal Analyst, Altimeter Group,
Author of *Engage!* and *The End of Business as Usual*

The sooner businesses learn that relationships are more important than ever, the sooner they can thrive. This book will help lead them down the road to success.

—C.C. Chapman, Author of *Content Rules* and *Amazing Things Will Happen*

The critical need to understand how to build and measure successful relationships has never been more important. In *Return on Relationship*, Ted Rubin and Kathryn Rose insightfully examine the intersection of digital technology and relationship marketing to deliver real value for brands.

—Linda Boff, Global Executive Director, Advertising and Digital Marketing, GE

Ted has teamed with Kathryn Rose and presented us with the book *Return on Relationship*. Discover how "relationships are the new currency" and put it into practice by reading this book!

—Ramon De Leon, Marketing Mind of Six Domino's Pizza stores in Chicago, Social Media Visionary, and Global Keynote Speaker

A must for the every employee to read. In *ROR*, Ted Rubin and Kathryn Rose use clear thinking, deep insight, and actual events to demonstrate how Return on Relationship is what defines and grows a brand today.

—Liz Strauss, International Social Business Strategist

Being successful in business has always started with the fundamental ability for us to build and nurture relationships with customers and prospects. Forget advertising, social media, direct mail, consumer behavior, and all that other stuff for just a moment and think about the foundation: relationships. Ted Rubin and Kathryn Rose help you get back to the foundation of business success with this book. It's a must-read for any business owner or business person, old or new.

—Jason Falls, Founder and CEO,
Social Media Explorer and co-author of
No Bullshit Social Media

Learning how to better your business through social media can be a daunting task. In *Return on Relationship*, however, authors Ted Rubin and Kathryn Rose write about the subject with candor and pragmatism. Whether you're a social media novice or a seasoned pro, you'll find their sage advice worth heeding.

—Mark Levy, Founder of Levy Innovation,
a marketing strategy firm for consultants
and other thought leaders

Ted Rubin and Kathryn Rose totally get relationship marketing. Finally a book that easily explains how to nail the real measure of your social media efforts.

—Tory Johnson, founder, Spark & Hustle,
and *New York Times* bestselling author

RETURN ON RELATIONSHIP

TED RUBIN AND KATHRYN ROSE

RETURN ON RELATIONSHIP

Relationships are the new currency: honor them,

invest in them, and start measuring your ROR

TATE PUBLISHING
AND **ENTERPRISES**, LLC

Published by Tate Publishing & Enterprises, LLC
127 E. Trade Center Terrace | Mustang, Oklahoma 73064 USA
1.888.361.9473 | www.tatepublishing.com

Tate Publishing is committed to excellence in the publishing industry. The company reflects the philosophy established by the founders, based on Psalm 68:11,
"The Lord gave the word and great was the company of those who published it."

Book design copyright © 2013 by Tate Publishing, LLC. All rights reserved.
Cover design by Joel Uber
Interior design by Jake Muelle

Published in the United States of America

ISBN: 978-1-62563-237-1
1. Business & Economics / E-Commerce / Internet Marketing
2. Business & Economics / Sales & Selling / General
13.01.03

ACKNOWLEDGMENTS

The content of this book is a concept that is near and dear to our hearts. Our journey to this book is truly a *Return on Relationship* story, and we are grateful that you've decided to join us. Both of us have considered ourselves *relationship marketers* long before the term became vogue and have built successful communities around brands using old-school methods like direct mail, in-person networking, and the telephone before the Internet and social media took hold. In these pages, we have made every effort to provide you with comprehensive ideas on how to use new tools and incorporate old ones to generate an endless supply of relationships that will help build and grow your business.

Special thanks to John Andrews for his belief in ROR and constant support, encouragement, and insight when Ted needed it most, and to the Collective Bias team for much of the same. Thank you also to Kathryn's clients, colleagues, and business partners for their understanding and support. The practice of ROR is how she is able to build communities that bring success to you and your campaigns.

We also want to thank some of the behind-the-scenes people who have helped us along the way: to our editor and friend, Apryl Parcher, we thank you for your wordsmithing and valuable suggestions on how to bring two people's ideas into one voice; Seth Longhurst, who designed a great site to promote the book, and Hanna Erlandsson, whom Ted counts on for support in all his social efforts. Other notable friends, colleagues, clients, and mentors whose ideas always inspire us include Seth Godin, C.C. Chapman, Mark Levy, Tamara Monosoff, Patty Farmer, Laura Rubinstein, Aaron Fertig, Shelley Ross, the late Kevin Aronin, and the blogging community whose support has been unwavering.

And last, but certainly not least, a very special thank you to our family and close friends. Ted's daughters have always been his inspiration, and what he learns from them he applies to all he does. Kathryn's parents and late grandmother, Rita, who taught her all about humility, gratitude, and the original concept of ROR, and her husband, Howard, and children, L.J. and Lorelei, for their love and patience; they always help her laugh and appreciate the little things in life.

The relationships we foster with our clients are modeled after the relationships we have with you. Thank you for giving your all. We will always strive to give you the return on relationship you deserve.

TABLE OF CONTENTS

FOREWORD

At PEMCO Insurance, our business model has long been one that leads with relationship. The voice of the customer and our ability to provide a truly "world class experience" at every opportunity has long been a top priority. Our goals include turning touch points into talking points and never having to advertise for a sales lead again. Several years ago, after materially differentiating our brand position and marketing campaign to one that's uniquely focused on the quirky tendencies and lifestyles of our Northwest neighbors, I was asked by a director on our board if the new campaign was working. My answer was a clear and resounding "yes!" "We're creating tons of smiles," I told him, "and smiles are the currency of conversations." Smiles lead to conversations, conversations to consideration, selection, renewal, referral, and advocates who are promoters and defenders of the brand. Ted Rubin and Kathryn Rose have taken a close look at the value that goes far beyond transactional dollars and cents. In *Return on Relationship*, the two have successfully put a bright light on the important conversations that C-level executives must have in order to be successful in today's market and highly socialized community. The answer goes far beyond social media tools and tactics. As Rubin and Rose discuss, a truly enabled and socially engaged enterprise is the answer. You'll want to read and apply the lessons they share within the pages of this book. I hope it makes you smile!

—Rod W. Brooks
Chief Marketing Officer, PEMCO
Mutual Insurance Company
Board Member, Word Of Mouth Marketing Association

.

INTRODUCTION

Relationships are the new currency...

The digital revolution has turned marketing on its head (or so some would have you believe). Just when you thought you had a handle on measuring ROI (Return on Investment), it seems that social media has thrown a monkey wrench in the whole business. But has it really?

In some ways it has because traditional formulas for calculating ROI really work better for advertising initiatives—and social is more about communication than it is about advertising. It's more about developing relationships and nurturing them, which oddly enough is almost a full circle back to the "before mass advertising" days of face-to-face sales and marketing. In those days, we actually met our customers, talked to them, and got to know them personally. What a novel concept!

Mass advertising (while it has its place) moved us away from our face-to-face roots, but social is bringing us back. It's how people today like to receive information and make buying decisions. They talk to each other via social channels. They seek information there, and they want to interact with businesses there directly or vicariously via the interaction of others. If you want to continue reaching your prospects in this social-media age, your marketing focus needs to return to building relationships.

Forget trying to tie traditional ROI metrics to social. After all, how do you measure the ROI of a conversation? In this book, we'll teach you how to rethink your social strategy in terms of its true value in ROR (Return on Relationship™).

ROR isn't a new concept in marketing; it's the value that accrues over time through loyalty, recommendations, and sharing. It's a back-to-basics measurement that calculates how well brands create authentic connection, interaction, and engagement with customers—and it's time to relearn the concept.

Between these pages, you'll learn how social marketing differs from traditional marketing, how to converse with and convert potential customers, and the importance of practicing persistence, patience, and brand humility. These may be watchwords of an earlier time, but we need to add them back to our business vocabulary in order to succeed today.

Relationships truly are the new currency in today's digital age. Get ready to dive in and find out how to make cultivation of those relationships a permanent part of your business culture.

Return on Relationship = ROI

CHAPTER ONE

YOUR FIELD OF DREAMS—IF YOU BUILD IT, WILL THEY COME?

> *"Build it and they will come" only works in the movies. Social Media is "build it, nurture it, engage them, and they may come and stay."*
>
> —Seth Godin

Unlike the iconic movie of the 1980s, *Field of Dreams*, it takes more than a "build it and they will come" mentality in order to succeed in social media. Loyal fans and followers don't just materialize out of thin air and flock to your profiles. Gaining the attention of the people you want to attract and getting them to engage with your brand is a constant work in progress—a field you should always be cultivating to achieve your goals.

Is your company creating a sense of community online? If not, you're missing something very important because it's relationships that bear fruit in today's social world. When brands actively try to cultivate good relationships—those built on trust, transparency and honesty—people respond. They naturally want to share their excitement about great products with their friends and the rest of their network. It's the way we're built as human beings.

However, we still find it amazing that in this time of social interaction exploding across the world, brands are still slow to embrace the idea of building communities. Too many are entrenched in old habits and try to make them fit in today's world. It just doesn't work. People are tired of one-way messaging, commercials, and advertisements being shoved at them from every direction. They would rather hang out with their friends online, share ideas, be entertained, and unwind, which is why social media evolved in the first place. It's a communication medium— not a platform for blast messaging and advertising. In order to use it effectively, you must build relationships and create a sense of community among your "followers" and "friends."

Social is quickly changing the way we need to think about brands and marketing. We can no longer expect to be successful if we just focus our efforts on telling our target market how great we are. The rules of the game have changed. What we, the brand, say about ourselves is no longer what matters. It's what *other* people say and the experiences they share about us that are important. You as a brand no longer control the conversation, and the sooner you wake up to that fact, the better off you'll be.

So in this new social age, what *do* brands have the power to control? Well, to a certain extent you can control your visual image—you can create a profile on a platform like Facebook or Twitter and have limited control of how the visitor sees your page. You control the content *you* use to communicate your brand message and also how that message is portrayed by you (but not how everyone else interprets it). And finally, you control how you react to people who post on your profile or reach out to you. But that's about it. The rest really depends on how well your message resonates with your audience's needs at the moment they see it. Will they "like" or "share" your message? Will they ask a question or comment? Building a social community around your brand depends on how well you attract people into conversation and how you interact with them, or how good you become at what is now called "relationship marketing."

RELEARNING HOW TO BUILD RELATIONSHIPS: A SHIFT IN MIND-SET

The fact that building relationships has only recently become the focal point of marketing seems a bit backward, as relationships should *always* be the focus of our interactions. However, up until the last decade, marketing has relied on a *Mad Men* mentality of convincing people to buy through the use of advertisements. The philosophy of "give the agency your creative ideas and let them come up with something" was the pervasive model back in the day, and it worked for years and years. However, social changed the marketing landscape forever, and those methods aren't going to survive—and neither will the brands that still cling to them.

Traditional advertising and marketing on one-way channels was about convincing people to buy your products, which sometimes included using catchphrases (remember "Where's the Beef?") or not-so-subtle comparisons to competitors' products. Because social is a two-way communication medium, brands need to shift away from the old one-way "convince and convert" thinking and move more in the direction of "converse and convert" to be successful on social channels.

Relationship marketing requires a twofold shift in mind-set. First, it requires an information-sharing outlook. People on social channels are looking for helpful, educational, or entertaining content that helps them make a buying decision. You can (and should) provide that for them, and the more the merrier. Website content, videos, podcasts, white papers, case studies—anything you can crank out. Any content that helps people understand your product or service and how to use it should be integrated into conversation via social media.

Secondly, it requires a willingness to take back the ownership of your brand voice rather than letting someone else come up with a catchphrase or AD copy. We no longer have the luxury of removing ourselves from the content creation and conversation—we have to be active in it. Plus, the conversation must continue after sales to reinforce customer relationships. However, this shift in mind-set is easier said than done because most brands are still fixated on ROI versus ROR and have a difficult time divesting themselves of the habit of viewing all marketing as "campaign-based."

Definition of ROR

ROR is the value that is accrued by a person or brand due to nurturing a relationship. ROI is simple dollars and cents, whereas ROR is the value (both perceived and real) that will accrue over time through loyalty, recommendations and sharing.

Many marketers don't want to invest time in this philosophy, even though published studies, such as Nielson's Trust and Advertising Global Report[1], show that people trust peer recommendations more than they do advertising. However, we have learned that the time investment is well worth it. Recommendations from friends have always been the best way to generate buzz and positive sentiment about a brand, but social media takes them to a whole new level, making them more visible and easier to share, so people are more likely to do it.

That doesn't mean that you should abandon traditional advertising. By all means, measure everything and keep what's working for you. It does mean that you need to understand that ROI thinking cannot be applied to social the same way it applies to traditional marketing.

So now that you understand the basic difference between the ROI mind-set and ROR thinking, are you ready to jump into high gear and develop an engaged social community around your brand? Not quite.

TWO MORE IMPORTANT FACTORS IN SHIFTING TO ROR

We've seen some big companies leap into social without taking into account a very important factor: their current brand perception in the marketplace. That's understandable; after all, social is relatively new on the marketing stage, so everyone's feeling their way. However, we have seen companies make big mistakes in two areas that affect brand perception in social circles: not integrating customer service and not creating an effective "Social ID." Both of these involve a further shift in mind-set and are absolutely critical to master—so let's dig in.

1. DEVELOPING A CUSTOMER SERVICE ATTITUDE

To many businesses, social media is still a campaign-based tactic, viewed and managed separately from business operations. This is flawed thinking. Social media marketing needs to be woven into the fabric of all marketing channels and strategically managed from a 360-degree perspective. Why? Because social communication has worked its way into most aspects of your customers' daily lives. There's no way around it—people who frequent social channels want the companies they deal with to interact with them on those channels.

Social integration is especially important around customer service, where the disparity between the customer experience in the social media channel and the customer experience in the traditional channel is a dangerous chasm. The result is a mixed message around customer service—an area where none of us can afford to be unclear or inconsistent.

To avoid this inconsistency, use social media for instant and ongoing engagement with your customers. Pay attention to them and address their needs early, often, and publicly. Make sure your social team and customer service team are on the same page and communicate regularly and easily. In short, make sure that communication doesn't taper off at any point. Both teams need to maintain their availability to the public, and they can't drop off after the sale is made.

So often we see that a brand or company is more than willing to put their name out there in the social sphere, but they don't seem to show up when someone has an issue or complaint. There isn't a worse time for a company to disappear, really, and if you keep the lines of communication open, you can turn a possible negative experience into a shining moment for your company. How? Simply by being there and taking an honest interest in what your customers have to say, even if it isn't good.

Responding publicly has another important, cost-saving benefit. Other people with the same issues (you can and should assume there are others) can receive resolution via your response. They see how you interact...and then make their own judgments about your brand character based on those interactions. If you're doing it right, you will build brand advocates in the process (more on brand advocates later).

Keeping constant contact with the customer isn't just advantageous in times of conflict or inquiry either. Engaging in a more personal way with your customers is also a good way to show what your company is made of; that is, individuals—people just like your customers. It's nice to see some humanity behind the giant talking head of a brand, so don't hide yours.

Dell does a good job with this on their Facebook page by having employees add their first name to any interactions with customers that posted on the wall. Although the thumbnail image is the recognizable blue Dell logo, people can always tell who is answering them.

Another brand that we've had experience with (and who gets the message) is Adobe. Ted recently had an issue downloading Photoshop for his teenage daughter and called the customer service line to no avail. So he immediately tweeted out his frustration, without even directly tagging Adobe, simply naming them in his tweet. Within fifteen minutes, he received responses from four different Adobe employees, with four different job functions, offering assistance! A product manager took the time, off hours, to set Ted up with technology support at a time when he would have access to his daughter's laptop. Needless to say, Ted is now an Adobe brand advocate and talks about them all the time.

As these examples illustrate, people who spend time on social media like to spend time with people—not logos. If you have a team of employees handling your social responses, don't make them hide behind the brand logo when they interact with followers—give them a voice and a face. Being able to see the team members behind the company and interacting with them personally makes a big difference in fan loyalty. It humanizes the brand and fosters good communication.

Transparency and *authenticity* are two of social media's most important watchwords, and that's why developing a good customer service attitude online (as well as within your organization) is so important. It's an essential part of your brand experience and ties in very closely with the next important factor in developing Return on Relationship, developing your brand's "social identification."

2. BUILDING YOUR SOCIAL ID

Brand identification is changing right along with the other shifts social media has brought about. It is no longer as much about the company logo, the colors, or whether we use our middle initial in visual materials or not; it is now about "Social ID"—our voice and the way we *socially* present ourselves online.

What is *your* Social ID? What identifies your brand (personal or corporate) throughout your social media interactions and offerings? If your answer includes the colors of your website, you need to think very carefully about where you are focusing your brand identity efforts. We're not suggesting that colors and logos and graphic elements are not important, but we *are* suggesting that the way you interact with others online is the brand identification factor that will catch the most attention…and hold it the longest.

So what specific actions does a Social ID include? No matter what your brand purpose is or what products and/ or services you provide, all of the following will influence your Social ID:

- ❑ Responsiveness: How responsive are you in your communications? Responding to inquiries, suggestions, and kudos should get as much attention as complaints do.
- ❑ Thought Leadership: How innovative are your ideas? Are you content to say what's already been said, or do you share your unique insights to provide real value to your audience?
- ❑ Content Creation: Are you just re-using the other guy's information, or are you creating new content, in new ways, that your audience can USE and re-use on your behalf?
- ❑ Relevance: Do you pay enough attention to your audience to know and provide what is relevant to them?
- ❑ Demeanor: How do you come across to your audience? Are your interactions friendly, helpful, gracious, and authentic, or do they suggest you are tired, annoyed, or not being genuine?

Every one of these areas is important because a positive Social ID fuels positive word of mouth and creates brand advocates. Your Social ID is about the interactive experience your audience has with you and your brand, and that experience is what your advocates will talk about—so make it positive!

What value are you providing for those with whom you interact? Think about it and make any changes you need so your Social ID works "for" you, not against you.

DON'T TRY TO RUSH IT: ROR TAKES TIME

Now that we understand the importance of building social relationships, how do we create those relationships quickly so we can move on to other things? We can't. And if we *want* to move on quickly away from a consumer relationship focus, we might as well not even make the effort.

Relationships take time and effort to build, and you must have a real desire to commit your resources to building and sustaining those consumer relationships. That's the only way you will see a high ROR.

By now you have an idea of how to make that shift in thinking, from an advertising mind-set to one of bringing value to your customers by providing them with rich content and authentic interaction rather than pitching them with sales messages. Next we'll discuss how you go about providing that value.

The following are three focus areas for building relationships online:

1. Relevance: No matter how perfectly or brilliantly worded your message is, it will not make an impact if the content itself doesn't matter to (*isn't relevant*

to) your audience. First think about and address what matters most to your audience. Give them a platform to show you what they need, want, are interested in, and expect. Whatever matters most to *them* should become what matters most to *you*!

2. Engagement: Start by asking relevant questions and proposing relevant ideas, and you can begin to engage your followers in such a way as to give them the ability and reason to respond. Then when they do respond, interact with them to solidify your relationship, lest it fade away. Directly acknowledge their response, ask follow-up questions, and share their insights with others.

3. Service: Ask your consumers, "How can I serve you?"—and mean it! They will recognize in a heartbeat if you are simply trying to *get* something from them, and they will not stick around. That's not to say that you can't promote something once in a while, but if you truly want to make an impact, aim to always put more energy and attention in your "give" column than in your "take" column. It *will* pay off.

Do you see a pattern emerging in how we're asking you to view your relationships with your customers? By now your mind should be buzzing with ideas on how to apply these concepts to your particular business model. We'll go into more detail in the next chapter, but here's a big-picture list of the things you'll need to be doing to develop ROR:

❑ Listen—Any social media campaign we begin for customers begins with a listening campaign. What are people saying about you, your brands, and your competitors? Formulating a Return on Relationship game plan is much easier when you know the players and positions.

❑ Find out what your constituency wants—Whom does your product or service serve, and how does it serve them? Taking the time to collect this important information will make it easier to determine what your market wants to hear about from you.

❑ Figure out where your market lives—Don't try to be everywhere. If your target market lives on Facebook and Twitter, spend 75 percent of your time there and 25 percent of the time on other channels.

❑ Learn the landscape, jargon, and etiquette of the tools you use—For example: don't post using hashtag (#) symbols on Facebook. The hashtag symbols are used on platforms like Twitter and Instagram, looks totally out of place on Facebook, and could alienate your audience.

❑ Be consistent and communicative—Many of the larger brands we have worked with still think that tweeting three times a week is a good strategy or that posting on Facebook twice a week will get them engagement. Not so. Learn to use the tools properly.

❑ Be responsive—Some bigger brands want to run every response through their legal department, which can bog response time down to days after someone posts a question. This is not how social media works, and brands that take this approach will not get the return they desire.

❑ Have disaster communication plan—You cannot please everyone, so take the time to figure out what you are going to say and how you are going to say it when the inevitable negative comment is written about you or your brand. Do not assume ignoring it will make it go away.

❑ Measure, measure, measure—Don't just measure numbers of fans and followers; measure the number of comments, shares, and retweets that your messages are receiving. Look at the demographics of your fans and followers. Are you reaching your target market?

❑ Tweak your efforts—It's important to realize that while a magazine AD or TV advertisement lasts weeks or months, you may need to tweak your social media strategy as much as daily if your message is not resonating. Thankfully, the immediacy of social makes that task much easier.

Keep these things in mind because they're essential to implementing a new mind-set that seeks to constantly engage with the customer rather than quantify his value from the outset. Forward-thinking companies are finding that they do better to concentrate on building relationships first. As it stands, there is no real way to put a dollar value on a bunch of people who "like" or "follow" your product. The real value is in the people who are the "super" fans or brand evangelists who market your product for you. Measurements like people talking about you on Facebook and watching for the RTs and mentions on Twitter are more likely to give you an idea of true value.

So far we've discussed the basics of how ROR works, and you should now have a clearer understanding of how to start broadening your marketing mind-set to include information sharing and customer service, taking back your brand voice, and building a Social ID. Those concepts are important in "preparing the ground" for cultivating productive relationships.

In this next chapter, we'll show you ways to sow the seeds of value that people are looking for in social channels. We'll also share some lessons learned from successful brand and personal relationship building and how to those apply to nurturing quality connections.

CHAPTER TWO

TAKE THEM TO DINNER FIRST

> *Dating is a give and take. If you only see it as "taking,"*
> *you are not getting it.*
>
> —Henry Cloud,
> author of *How to Get a Date Worth Keeping*

START WITH A COURTSHIP

All relationships start with a courtship period, and relationship marketing is no different—yet it's surprising how many marketers have forgotten the etiquette of dating when it comes to building relationships. The art of getting to know people and taking a relationship one step at a time has become lost.

In fact, Seth Godin, who popularized the term *permission marketing*, once remarked at a conference that a typical online marketing program often resembles a *really* bad dating strategy. He outlined a scenario in which a guy walks into a bar and asks the first women he sees to marry him. If the woman doesn't accept, he asks the next and the next and the next—until he's proposed to every woman in the room. He then goes to another bar, and a few more, and repeats this process until someone actually accepts his proposal.

Sounds silly, doesn't it? Yet this is exactly what marketers do when they constantly shout out the same offer over and over again in an attempt to get their message in front of millions of eyeballs.

Too many brands assume that the most effective way to market in this digital age is to use social media to post and tweet as many marketing messages as possible to the widest range of potential consumers across the greatest number of social networks. Spread the word to anyone and everyone, and hope someone believes enough in your message to create a connection and become an advocate influencer for your brand.

Just as in Seth Godin's dating example, this "spray and pray" strategy doesn't work in building relationships online. In fact, it's one of the fastest ways to build negative sentiment around your brand (you'll get a lot of virtual drinks thrown in your face!). Get to know your audience and identify those who might be a good match first. Approach gently. Ask permission to have a conversation. Listen more than you speak. Don't try to cut to the chase until you've asked them out to dinner first—in fact, take them out to dinner *a lot*.

Your social audience doesn't owe you their attention. You have to earn it, and that's not done with a gimmick or a flashy set of ads. Why do you think the "no call" list and anti-spam laws were put into effect? The more connected people are, the more they need to protect their space—and the more selective they are about the information they choose to absorb. Just because you're sitting in a bar doesn't mean you want to spend your time fending off unwanted advances.

Social media platforms are no different, and in fact, social marketing is the ultimate in permission marketing as Seth Godin defines it:

> Permission marketing is the privilege (not the right) of delivering anticipated, personal and relevant messages to people who actually want to get them.

So how do we earn our social audience's permission? We must first start with developing a deep understanding of their preferences and needs and not trying to control the conversation. Remember, you're not advertising here—you're dating! And like a good date (versus the date from hell), you need to develop consideration for your partner(s). Here are some examples:

1. Telling versus Listening: It may sound counterintuitive, but if you truly want to be heard above the growing social media "noise," you need to *listen*. Listen to what your audience and potential consumers are saying before you even put one word out there: What are they saying, what are they feeling, what are their pain points, and what solutions do they need? Then when you do "speak," empathize with them and ask them questions.

2. Me versus You: Do you come from a "*me*" perspective and speak first about your brand, product, or service,

or do you come from a "*you*" perspective and first address what matters most to your consumer (their needs, wants, interests, and expectations)? Whatever matters most to your audience should become what matters most to you!

3. "What can you give me?" versus "How can I serve you?": Taking the "*me*" mentality one step further, when we are *advertising* instead of *building relationships*, we are focused on what our audience can give us instead of how we can best serve them.

4. Instant Impact versus Ongoing Engagement: Traditional advertising is going for instant impact and hoping and praying you make an impression: splashy billboards, off-the-wall Super Bowl television ads, eye-catching graphics, even shock factor (images of gore, poverty, nudity, animal cruelty, etc.). While those methods are effective in catching a consumer's attention, they fall short of *retaining* that attention.

   Building relationships, in contrast, is about starting meaningful dialogue and taking the time to thoughtfully and genuinely engage in ongoing conversation. Relationships focus on getting to know your audience and giving them reasons to stay engaged—not just getting them to react.

5. Where is the Money? versus Who are the People? Short and simple: if you are only focused on the money, you risk completely overlooking the people. Don't make that mistake! If you don't know who *your* people are, you might as well toss your marketing

money down the drain. Who are the people you want to attract, and why?

The key to all this is listening first. You can't develop a deep understanding of what your audience wants without listening, just as you cannot develop a truly meaningful personal relationship without listening. You have to be willing to get out of your own way and stop thinking of what you're going to say next in a conversation.

YOUR BRAND IS ALL ABOUT *THEM*

We marketers like to think that social media is primarily a set of tools for our marketing purposes, but in reality, social media is also a strong set of tools our consumers use to share and influence opinion about our brand. Consumers' opinions now create the "reality" of the brand. In essence, consumers now own your brand, and if enough consumers say negative things about it, you lose credibility.

If you fight to retain control, you're likely to hold on so tightly that you suffocate the flexibility and outward-looking awareness your organization needs for survival in today's market. This whole notion of ceding brand ownership to the consumer may be uncomfortable, but it presents a great opportunity. If you're willing to step into their world and listen to them, your audience can (and will) tell you how they expect your products to work and what they expect from you. This allows you to build the kind of brand your audience wants rather than what you *think* they want. When you listen to your consumers as though they are brand owners, you're showing them respect—and in this social media world, authentic respect is one of the greatest customer experiences we can provide.

Thanks to the continual evolution of social media, we have a growing set of useful tools for listening to conversations and gathering feedback about our brand reputation. Online branded communities are increasingly valuable meeting spaces where community members and brand marketers can easily engage in meaningful conversation around specific products and services…especially private forums where the communications are protected and lend a feeling of comfort for both the consumer and the brand.

Once such community is Social Fabric®, a private online community owned by Collective Bias™, the leading social shopper media company and where Ted serves as Chief Social Marketing Officer. The community consists of over 1,400 members and brands and over 200 interest groups.

Social Fabric members join interest groups within the community and apply for opportunities they feel passionate about. Collective Bias sends these members into stores to purchase product and show their entire path-to-purchase experience with the brand. They call these opportunities "shoppertunities," and the entire process is documented using social sharing applications and various social media applications.

However, members don't just participate in shopping campaigns—they also assist in the brainstorming and planning process. In fact, client brands have round-the-clock access to this community of influencers. They can interact, engage, ask questions, get opinions, and learn from those who are not only their target consumer but who also interact with their own audiences regularly and have their fingers in the pulse of what is most important to brands.

Other places to go for "listening" include:

- ❑ Facebook
- ❑ Twitter search
- ❑ YouTube
- ❑ Customer surveys
- ❑ Both paid and free sentiment-measurement tools such as:

  - ◄ Radian 6
  - ◄ Sentiment Metrics
  - ◄ Strutta
  - ◄ Mutual Minds
  - ◄ Twendz
  - ◄ Social Mention

Once you start this listening process, you'll see where conversations are happening about your brand and discover opportunities for engaging in those conversations and finding out more about what your audience wants. In fact, the amount of brand-consumer conversation going on now in the social space has changed consumer expectations. When your audience sees that you are part of their communities, they assume that you're listening, hearing, and planning product and service changes accordingly.

REDISCOVERING BRAND HUMILITY

Talking about listening is all well and good, but are you really hearing? Sometimes we are so committed to our own brand experience that we have trouble actually hearing when our consumers are trying to ask us to change. In order to work around that (natural and understandable) resistance, we need to take a step back from our fierce attachment to what we believe makes our brand successful and learn to be humble again. In other words, we must get out of our own way and rebuild our brand assessment from the eyes of the consumer (remember, it's all about them!).

How do we do this? One of the best ways is to pretend you're a start-up, and use what you learn in your listening campaign to build a consumer-based brand assessment:

1. Gather feedback about your product, service, or brand as though it were in the very earliest stages of development or as if you were your own competition, trying to build a powerful product, service, or brand based completely on consumer feedback.
2. Create a complete description of the finished product, service, or ideal brand experience (based on #1).
3. Compare the "new" description with your current product, service, or brand, noting any areas where your existing offering falls short of the "new" description.
4. Create an action plan to address specific changes needed in your current product, service, or brand.

In short, send your ego to the back seat, and bring your consumers to the front. It's much easier to hear what your audience wants when you get your own biases and preconceived notions out of the way. When you adopt a marketing philosophy centered on relearning humility and building relationships, things really start to happen. Consumers who feel truly valued, who feel that you're really listening and taking to heart their needs and desires, will in turn assign value to your brand by buying your product/ service and passing recommendations on to their networks. The sale then becomes a natural part of the ROR instead of a "hard sell" effort.

MAKE THEM FEEL SPECIAL

Just as with a courtship, once you learn your audience's likes and dislikes and what they're looking for in a relationship, you can work on creating experiences for them that make them feel appreciated. In social circles, your connections feel appreciated when you acknowledge them as individuals. Here are some socially oriented ideas:

❏ Give shout-outs: Tag the person in a public update with a short statement of why you value them.

❏ Send them a picture or helpful article: Post a picture or article link on the person's personal profile or e-mail it to them and say something like, "I saw this and thought of you, (give their name)."

❏ Give a recommendation or testimonial: If your customer has a LinkedIn profile and you're connected, send them a spontaneous recommendation (without asking for one in return).

☐ Klout influence: If you know people in the Klout. com network, add them as influencers or give them +Ks in their area of expertise to help their Klout scores. Even if you do not believe in what Klout does and how they do it, recognizing others will always have value.

Don't forget about showing appreciation outside social channels as well. For instance, you could develop a practice of sending thank-you cards to your mailing list when seasons change. We don't often receive cards in the mail these days, so they get our attention. A nice card that says, "Thank you for being such a great [friend, customer, client, etc.], we hope you're enjoying the spring weather!" is sure to give the recipient a lift.

Birthday cards are another example. Everyone likes receiving birthday cards. If you can hand write them and stamp them, so much the better. In fact, personally acknowledging any kind of life event with a card is a good practice, whether it's a positive event or sympathy for a loss. It helps us feel more connected.

Remember, reaching out to show appreciation should never be a chore—it should become a habit. The more you do it, the more natural it becomes, and the more fun you'll have with it. Plus, the relationships you nourish with this attention will grow to be priceless and add significantly to your Return on Relationship.

FIND AND CULTIVATE YOUR BRAND ADVOCATES

Earlier we mentioned the importance of developing brand advocates to help spread the good word about your organization. But what is a brand advocate, and how do you identify them?

One of the best definitions (or set of them) we've found for brand advocacy was put forward by Zuberance, an award-winning social media marketing company.

> A Brand Advocate is a highly satisfied customer or other* who recommends their favorite brands and products without being paid to do so.
>
> —Zuberance

Brand advocates don't have to be customers per se—they can be people who are noncompetitive peers in the marketplace, or someone who just admires your company because they like your philosophy and can identify with it.

So how do you find potential brand advocates among your followers and friends? And more importantly, how can you nurture and energize them?

One successful big-brand example of empowering advocates from their consumer base was the Kleenex "Softness Worth Sharing" campaign[2]. In this "social sampling" campaign, the Kimberly-Clark Corp. brand let people send samples of their new softer tissues to family and friends via signups at participating retailers in the United States and Canada. They could also send virtual

Kleenex tissues to Facebook friends. The campaign rolled out across Kleenex's print, digital and social advertising, and participants could track online how their samples inspired others to follow suit.

The campaign quickly went viral, resulting in over 1.5 million shares of the product—a true success story in brand advocacy. When consumers can see the impact of their action, it can easily inspire them to act again and spread the word to their friends about this "cool thing you have to check out!" It energizes and mobilizes advocates. Kleenex made it easy and fun for advocates to create a buzz around a specific product and to share the experience of the product—not just talk about it. Successful social sampling campaigns like this rely on consumer-to-consumer connection, and your advocates are the most powerful way to create those ties.

The Kleenex campaign is a good example of consumer-focused advocacy, but what about B2B? Examples of nonconsumer advocates could be those in your own peer networks. Do you belong to a lead referral group (physical) or an engaged group on LinkedIn or Facebook? Once you get to know the members in those groups and network with them, relationship-building opportunities begin to occur. The key there is actually getting to know each other and taking communication beyond the casual acquaintanceship stage. Make it a part of your day to regularly reach out to peers in your networks. Pick up the phone; offer to grab a coffee together; have a Skype conversation. Think of ways you can refer business to them or recommend them to your network. Developing close ties with peers can be a great source of referrals for you. When someone wants to know what service provider to use or which brand provides the most consistently performing product at a price that meets their budget, where do they turn? They ask their friends, relatives, and colleagues…and even people they don't know but still trust simply because they are part of their extended social network. The key here is that another individual—not a brand promising perfection via one of its ads—recommended your service or product.

Recommendations are more likely to lead to action (a purchase or passing on the recommendation, for example) due to their interpersonal nature, and also because recommendations are often requested with the intent to purchase. Therefore, it's our job as marketers to facilitate and nurture relationships that lead to recommendations—another form of brand advocacy.

ADVOCACY BEGINS WITH GREAT PRODUCT/SERVICE: DOES YOURS PASS THE SOCIAL Q.C. TEST?

Before you get all excited about advocates, however, it's important to note that quality control of your product or service is paramount in order to pass muster with them. The above Kleenex product is a good example. Their customers found it to indeed be "soft enough to share," or the campaign would not have achieved the result it did. In other words, it passed their advocates' Social Q.C. test.

If your product is fantastic, your advocates will spread the word like wildfire. Social networks and traditional word of mouth will start buzzing with your product, and sales will reflect your advocates' delight.

But your advocates won't try to get someone to buy a sub-par product, and they certainly won't apologize for you. Don't try to make your advocates do that work for you because they won't…and they shouldn't have to. True advocacy starts by building a foundation of trust. People will go out of their way to buy and recommend products and services that don't require an apology, so make sure that what you offer is everything you promised. If you don't deliver what's expected, essential trust is quickly lost, along with the sale.

You might be tempted to use social media to over-highlight the best parts of your product in the hopes that the disappointing parts won't be noticed. But even the best social media relationships can't perform magic, so don't waste your time trying to hide product flaws. Invest your time in making a flawless product and providing great service, and give your advocates something to get excited about! The good news is that when your product is strong and does carry through on your brand promises, advocates, through their social media relationships, can skyrocket your sales. Advocates engage, word gets out, and sales happen. They will go out of their way for you because they want to…because your product is what it is supposed to be and passed your advocates' Social Q.C. test.

In addition to ensuring that your product or service is of the highest quality, you must also carefully nurture those who go out of their way to further your brand. Earlier we mentioned that you should be thinking of ways to make your audience feel special. This is even more important with those you identify as brand advocates. Think of them as your very best customers. However, keep in mind that "best customer" in this instance isn't necessarily the one who provides the most money the quickest. Relationship value isn't measured in how much your advocates can bring you in immediate monetary gain but in the relationships they build for you in terms of numerous referrals, repeat business, and overall positive brand impact over time. Always be thinking of ways to build strong relationships with them:

- ❑ Pay even more attention to them: watch, listen, learn
- ❑ Get to know their preferences so you can continue to delight them
- ❑ Go "above and beyond" in your interactions with them
- ❑ Solicit their honest feedback at key brand or product development decision points
- ❑ Go out of your way to make sure they know you appreciate them (their insights, time, energy, loyalty)
- ❑ Be hyper-aware of their value
- ❑ Invite them to visit with you online, and welcome their friends as warmly as you welcome them
- ❑ Think more often in terms of ways you can *serve* them better instead of how they can serve you

Treat your advocates as partners in building your brand. When you do, they will become stronger and more loyal, resulting in the holy grail of advocacy—higher customer lifetime marketing value.

In this chapter, we've talked about the importance of taking a more personal interest in your online relationships and viewing people not as advertising objects but as individuals to be courted with "permission marketing." We also discussed the concept that social media has switched brand ownership into the hands of the consumer, as well as some ideas on developing and fostering brand advocacy and loyalty—all important concepts to master for higher ROR.

Now that we understand how relationships need to change, let's focus on where to go to look for those relationships—and what language we need to be speaking in order to be heard.

CHAPTER THREE

DETERMINE YOUR PRODUCT'S SOCIAL MARKET

> *The aim of marketing is to know and understand the customer so well the product or service fits him and sells itself.*
>
> —Peter F. Drucker

When you listen to your audience, get to know them, and spend time discovering what they want, you'll have a better idea what to share with them and how to communicate. But where is your market in the social space? Who's looking for your product or service on which channel, and how do we provide information to them that they'll find relevant to their lives?

We'll go into a little more detail on several of the various social platforms and the type of people that reside in them in this chapter, but first let's talk about relevancy. It goes way beyond advertising demographics. Relationship building takes more into account, so in order to formulate relevant content that will capture your audience's attention, you first need to take a closer look at who they are as individuals.

CREATING PERSONAS

When we ask clients the question "who are you trying to target?" many times we get the standard old-school marketing broad demographic answers such as "women 25-54, upper level income." When your ultimate goal is to build relationships, you have to go much deeper than that.

One of the greatest benefits of today's social media and online marketing opportunities is that you can really target your audience down to their interest levels, zip codes, what TV shows they watch, and more, simply because they tell the social networks what they like, and they talk about these things in their bios, tweets, and online interactions.

In Kathryn's book, *Solving the Social Media Puzzle: 7 Simple Steps to Planning a Social Media Marketing Strategy for Your Business*, she dedicates an entire chapter to building "personas," or snapshots of the kind of person who makes up your ideal market. This includes giving the person a name, a face, and building out a personal profile of that person.

Building personas, as opposed to using simple demographics, is a practice that's gaining steam among mainstream marketers as well. In fact, NBC News Digital recently began using personas to target advertising to television news audiences, and their research led them to develop four distinctly different persona types. In an interview with Online Media Daily[3] unveiling the new persona-based targeting concept, Kyoo Kim, Vice President of Sales at NBC News Digital, said they were shifting to personas "because focusing on behavior versus demographics gives our customers better insights into the tendencies of our viewers."

Since your business probably has several target markets and subcategories within them, like NBC News, you can build a different persona for each target because the kind of content that appeals to one may not be relevant to another—and they may also reside on different social channels. Your high-level brand message might be somewhat relevant to a broader audience, but the more precisely your message matches an audience's interests/ needs, the more value each consumer will perceive from your brand. For example, if your brand offers various products across several categories, don't assume that anyone in your audience is equally interested in all of your offerings.

In social channels, the more complete your persona profiles, the better, so both your content *and* conversations have a better chance of resonating. When you can picture someone in your mind, it's easier to strike up a one-on-one conversation with them—something that's very valuable in communication. And the more relevant you can be, the greater your likelihood of developing high ROR. Think through and assess how to be relevant for each product and each particular audience so you can provide content that creates that bond and interaction.

Once you've determined who your audience is, their affinity for your product or service, and the kind of information they are looking for, the next step is finding out where to look for those people in the social space.

WHERE DO YOUR PERSONAS LIVE?

Twitter, Facebook, LinkedIn, Pinterest—which platform is best for your particular market? Is there one in particular that your ideal audience prefers, or do they frequent several platforms? Which platform will give you the biggest bang for your buck?

There are lots of questions you could ask in order to pin this down more closely, but now that you've done some listening and built out your personas, it may be helpful to get a sense of the top four platforms and the kind of people who frequent them so you can get a sense of where your targets live. The figures below were gathered using Quantcast, a team of web analytics experts, and OnlineMBA.com.

FACEBOOK

Of the over 140 million U.S. people on Facebook every month, users are generally:

❑ Female (same ratio as Twitter)
❑ Young adults (18-34, although 45-54 year olds make up 11%)
❑ Have kids (57%)
❑ More affluent (32% earn more than $150K, and 30% earn between $100 and $150K)
❑ No college (47% don't hold a degree, but 40% have some college)
❑ Ethnicity (while 73% of users are Caucasian, African Americans are over-indexed, followed by Asians)

Lifestyle interests[4] range from communities, politics, and news to home décor and food.

LINKEDIN

LinkedIn is used by more than thirty-eight million people monthly. Contrary to Twitter and Facebook, LinkedIn skews a little differently in its demographic makeup:

- ❑ Male (51% as opposed to 49% Female)
- ❑ Middle-Aged (45-54 year olds make up 21% of the base, with 35-44 year olds at 22%)
- ❑ No kids (Since this demographic is a little older, it makes sense that 56% have no children in the household. However, 44% still have kids at home)
- ❑ More affluent (here again, a significant segment of the LinkedIn populace earns more than $150K)
- ❑ Higher education (More than half of LinkedIn users have graduate or post-graduate degrees)
- ❑ Ethnicity (79% Caucasian, but Asians represent a higher index in this platform)

Lifestyle interests not included for this profile.

YOUTUBE

With more than 161 million users monthly, YouTube is a dominant force in social media. The demographics represented are as follows:

- ❑ Gender (Equal in ratio 50% each)
- ❑ Young adult (The younger audience under 18 to 34 predominates at 26 and 20%, but older audiences also use the platform)
- ❑ Have kids (More than half the audience has children)
- ❑ More affluent (Largest segment has income over $150k, but those with lower incomes are represented also)
- ❑ No college (Half the audience does not have a college education "yet")
- ❑ Ethnicity (The Hispanic audience shows a heavy index after Caucasian)

It's not surprising that lifestyle interests[5] in this group tend to be centered around video primarily, with politics, humor, and news following closely.

PINTEREST

According to OnlineMBA.com[6], approximately 1.36 million people use Pinterest on a daily basis, with the following demographic profile:

- ❑ Gender (Predominantly female—over 80%)
- ❑ Adult (Age groups 25-34 are most highly represented)
- ❑ Have kids (50% of users have children)
- ❑ More affluent (More than 28% of users are well off, with $100k+ income)
- ❑ Higher education (Approximately 61% of users have a college degree)
- ❑ Ethnicity (not measured)

Lifestyle interests include crafts, gifts, hobbies, interior design, fashion, and food.

TWITTER

What kind of people use Twitter? The platform has over ninety million monthly users in the U.S., who fall into these general categories:

- ❑ Female (55%—versus 45% male)
- ❑ Young adults (highest usage among 18-34 year-olds)
- ❑ Have kids (55% of users have children in the household)
- ❑ More affluent (30% earn $150K+)
- ❑ No college (49% don't hold a college degree)
- ❑ Ethnicity (65% of users are Caucasian, but African Americans and Hispanics are over-indexed, which means that Twitter attracts a more concentrated group of these ethnic groups than the general Internet population)

Quantcast also determined that the above audience also has a variety of lifestyle interests[7], from politics and commentary to home and gardening.

OUR TAKE ON TWITTER:
IT'S NOT JUST ANOTHER PLATFORM

Many people misunderstand the current power and relevant scale of Twitter, and it's not about how Twitter has scaled to the general public. The most important thing about news, content, and anything else published via Twitter is that a great deal of the influencer community is utilizing Twitter for news, communication, and discovery. It's a tool that leads into other forms of social sharing because information first shared on Twitter finds its way to other publishing mediums such as blogs, traditional news media, Facebook, Pinterest, Google+, the office water cooler, or whatever other mediums exist.

We consider Twitter a place to lay the groundwork where other people pick up things. It's a seeding medium. That means it's not about the quantity of people listening at once but about the ability to lay it out there for those whose attention are drawn to what you have to say at any given moment. When those seeds are sprouted, they spread from there.

This all happens in real time, so Twitter enables news and information to spread very quickly, often from the source—and the information then gets shared and edited to reflect the views and insights of those sharing.

The above list is just a starting point, so use it as a guide to begin your search for ideal platforms. Of course, there are many more social platforms, and more created every day. You cannot possibly hope to manage representation on a large number of them. The bottom line is that different platforms will come and go, but the need to connect and build relationships with our audience members will only grow stronger. The trick is to choose those where your ideal audience and their interests are well represented. That might take a little research. So before you grab at the next shiny new social media toy that takes the world by storm, take some time to check out who's actually visiting and communicating there. Facebook and Twitter might be in use right now, but facts and figures change—so keep an eye out.

The main questions to ask yourself (and your team) when considering social channels are:

❑ How complex will it be for us to establish and maintain a presence here?

❑ Are our top competitors represented here as well? How are they doing?

❑ Do the interests of most users here match those of our audience persona(s)?

❑ How likely are we to build the best relationships with users of this platform?

Remember, you don't have to be everywhere at once. We've found that it's better to concentrate on one or two platforms than to spread your brand presence too thin on half a dozen. If you are running low on time or staff, make a list of the possible platforms, decide which of these will best serve your needs, and attract the audience you desire. Focus your efforts on that one or two for the next ninety days, and then add others as you have time.

Also keep in mind that the persona profiles you created at the beginning of this chapter should be living, breathing documents. People grow, change, and switch preferences. Make sure you revisit your personas, talk to your customer-facing employees about them, and tweak them as needed. They're great tools to use in planning your core content as well as ongoing social conversation, so keep them up to date.

CHAPTER FOUR

CONVERSE AND CONVERT

Most of us hear okay; however, few of us listen well.
—Lillian D. Bjorseth,
author of *Shhh! Listen, Don't Just Hear*

Okay, now that you've learned how to court your market and find out where they like to hang out in the social space, it's time to concentrate on conversing with them. Let's assume that you have a branded profile on a platform or two and you're starting to a responsive community on those platforms. Perhaps you've started to identify some potential brand advocates as well, and that's a good thing. The hard part is keeping it up and not falling back into old habits, so in this chapter we'll give you some pointers on nurturing your followers and avoiding some of the pitfalls that can derail relationship building.

BEWARE OF THE ADVERTISING TRAP

Most companies develop platforms on social media with the goal of increasing sales. However, if you've been paying attention, you've also seen some pushback from social audiences who view active marketing on social channels as an intrusion into their social conversations. Also Facebook's social graph made a lot of people nervous about what companies could find out about them. Many voiced the concern that Facebook would sell their information to companies that would stalk them to sell them "more stuff."

Marketers have to understand that most people are just not very receptive to direct selling while being social. Yes, we all like to hear about things from our friends, associates, acquaintances, but that doesn't mean we're in a commerce frame of mind when those interactions take place.

Now we're not talking about ads here. There's a legitimate use for advertisements on social channels, and people expect to see those advertisements, or at least understand why they are there—but people *don't* want a company to actively pitch them in their newsfeed or stream. When companies actively market to their connections in this way, we call it the "advertising trap." It's a fine line you don't want to cross.

For instance, the Insight Strategy Group conducted a survey[8] early in 2012 of 514 adults from 18 to 64 years of age who previously or currently had an account on a social networking site such as Facebook, LinkedIn, Twitter, Foursquare, or YouTube. The vast majority (94 percent) of those surveyed understood that companies used social to get in front of potential customers, but a whopping 64 percent stated that they "hate when a company finds them through their social networking profile," and almost 60 percent found it invasive when companies used social networking because they consider their social profiles to be for "people socializing."

However, over half of those surveyed by Insight Strategy said they wanted companies to have a page or feed on social platforms and that they considered those pages to be the best places to deliver feedback to companies.

If that sounds fickle, well…it is. But what it tells us is that people like to be in control of their social experience. They know where the ads are going to show up and can choose to ignore them or click on them if the product is interesting to them or fits their needs at the moment. They'll view a company page to get information, find out about deals that interest them, ask a question, or raise a complaint—but the control must be from their end. They want information and conversation—not pitches.

In an article on Inc.com, "Is Your Social Media Marketing a Turnoff?[9]" author Eric Sherman gives some further insight:

> When a company has a page on Facebook or a Twitter feed that provides information about deals, the consumer remains in control, fitting in with her observations. You go to the page or feed when you want to get something of value, or to raise a complaint.
>
> Now have a company actively market to consumers via social networks. It's as though the business broke into people's online homes to sell them its new bar of soap. That sort of active marketing becomes the literal embodiment of following consumers where they go online. Only, instead of quietly watching from the edges…the

company now jumps into view to deliver a pitch. Put that way and it seems downright creepy.

REMEMBER TO *BE SOCIAL*

So now you know that overt pitching, as a regular practice, is a bad idea. What else *doesn't* work for a social media strategy? Not being *social*. It might sound like common sense, but all too often being social is overlooked in a social media strategy. It's not enough to just start accounts with all the most popular social media tools and community sites, even when you include professionally designed graphics and a big, bold display of your logo and a few text lines about your brilliant mission. First and foremost, you absolutely must be social—but what does that mean?

Well, it means actively initializing conversation, putting information out there, asking questions, sharing pictures, and interacting with people at every opportunity. If people don't hear from you, if you're not tweeting or updating or messaging at all—if you're just lurking in the space and there are crickets chirping on your social profiles—you're not being social. Being silent online isn't good because even if you think there is no message, you *are* sending a message to your consumers and potential consumers that you don't want to socialize. From the consumer perspective, that looks like this:

- ❑ Not paying attention
- ❑ Not being interested

- ❏ Not caring
- ❏ Not engaging and interacting

When you are silent online, you are actually screaming, "We don't want to make the effort to build relationships or pay attention!"

There is pressure these days to have a perfect social media strategy in place and to have it in place *now*. A carefully thought-out, integrated strategy is very important, but even more important right now is to just start being social by:

- ❏ Being genuinely interested ... and interest*ing*
- ❏ Paying consistent attention to your consumers
- ❏ Asking questions, responding to answers, asking more questions, responding again (i.e. *engage*)
- ❏ "Talking" *with* your consumers, not *at* them
- ❏ Providing real, relevant value by interacting, listening, and socializing

Start now. Be social while you're honing your strategy and building your ideal social team so when you implement the rest of your strategy, your consumers will already be gathered around you.

IT'S CALLED NETWORKING FOR A REASON

You can have a killer website, a great-looking Facebook page, Twitter and YouTube branding—the works. But if you're not reaching out to comment on other people's posts, sharing other people's good content, actively helping where you can, and generally joining in the conversation on these channels, then what you're doing is like sitting on the side of a busy highway with a "Please Like Me" sign over your head. Lots of luck with that.

Getting people to follow your profiles isn't all that difficult, but if you want more from your social media activities, then give your customers and prospects a reason to take the time out of their busy lives to "listen" to you. They're looking for answers to their questions, solutions to their problems, and they're also looking to make real, one-on-one connections with real people (Hint: It's called networking). Many now see networking, due the plethora of platforms offering connections, as simply clicking a button and connecting virtually. But what networking really means is getting to know people.

For instance, traditional networking groups are a prime example of physical, one-on-one networking that really works. By making a commitment to show up to weekly meetings with fellow business owners, listening to their needs, and making a concerted effort to bring them referrals and help them get more customers, participants gain referrals in return. It's called a "giver's gain" philosophy because the amount of referrals they get tends to correlate directly to the amount of "giving" they do, which requires them to develop relationships with each other and develop trust. Those that attend only talk endlessly about themselves don't last long; it's the deep relationships that develop over time that really produce results.

Developing fruitful relationships in social channels works exactly the same way and takes the same amount of dedication and work:

- ❑ Get to know your customers/prospects by actively listening to their needs in social channels
- ❑ Reach out to others without waiting for them to "like" you first
- ❑ Contribute to conversations where you can provide value (not a sales pitch)
- ❑ Always be thinking of ways to help others solve problems
- ❑ Introduce people when appropriate
- ❑ Be genuine in your responses and outreach
- ❑ Don't expect reciprocation, but always strive to give it when someone reaches out to you

In many ways, networking on social channels is like going back to our roots as physical networkers. Both are about building relationships. However, those who take themselves out of the equation and focus on the needs of others can expect to get a better Return on Relationship™.

DEVELOPING BRAND ADVOCATES: GET YOUR CUSTOMERS' HELP

But how do you develop awareness around your product or service when the stream is so busy you can't get a word in edgewise? Here's one often-overlooked resource in amplifying your message online: consumers. And not just any consumers, your own customers!

Whether you are a retailer or your market is B2B, your consumers are always on the lookout for validation, especially if you're selling the same thing as the brand down the street. Why should they buy from you versus them? Believe it or not, the customers you already have can help you out with this—and all you have to do is ask.

But this is where a lot of companies fall down when using social. They get so tied up in the parameters of the platform that they forget to think outside it. They sink money into platform advertising, contests, and mobile apps to attract new followers but forget completely to tap the one source that could exponentially increase their reach...the people who have already bought from them!

Remember, brand advocacy doesn't come from advertising spend or buying followers via any other social mechanism. It comes from people sharing their experiences with your brand via their networks. So how do you get them to do this?

The brand Zaggora does it by going after what they call "ambassadors" of their HotPants™ women's exercise clothing and rewarding them for sharing their stories. If you take a look at their website, you can see that they've got some press going, a magazine they share with their growing e-mail list, and also a healthy Facebook presence, all of which is focused on leveraging the customer's story. Zaggora understands that their market wants to hear how others have achieved success, lost inches, or gained strength before they spend their money—so they've pulled out the stops to create a great customer experience and reward their ambassadors for spreading the word. It works like magic.

B2B companies can tap into the same power. In fact, according to customer advocacy data from the Zuberance. com blog, 50 percent of B2B customers are highly likely to recommend a service or product to their networks, 30 percent of advocates recommend the first time they're given an opportunity, and a whopping 70 percent of those advocates' contacts respond to recommendations.

Once you identify these folks, reach out to them! Think of ways you can thank them for sharing your content or recommending your brand. Remember, your customers have a wide array of networks, so look for potential brand evangelists wherever you have a connection, not just on social channels. Mine your e-mail list, tap into the influence of bloggers, pick up the phone and call them, speak to customers in your place of business—find them wherever you can!

THE TRUE VALUE OF "SHARE" VERSUS "LIKE"

As we talk about brand advocacy, it's important to note that just as one-time customers aren't as valuable as repeat buyers, the casual social follower, liker, or subscriber isn't as valuable as those who actively share your message with their networks. So how do you turn more of your casual social likers and followers into brand ambassadors?

Each social platform has different parameters, but let's take Facebook as an example. In a blog post in socialmediaexaminer.com entitled "9 Facebook Marketing Strategies to Build Super Fans[10]," Facebook marketing expert and author Amy Porterfield outlines nine ways to build engagement that creates brand advocacy among Facebook audiences.

In the article, she explains how to move people from light to heavy engagement, and we find it interesting that the first two things she covers are humanizing the platform and listening to your audience. She's right on the money there because as we've discussed, people want to deal with people, and they're tired of messaging that doesn't resonate with their individual needs. The rest of the strategies discussed in the article, such as fostering communication (between you and your fans as well as fan to fan), making word-of-mouth sharing easy and fun, being deliberate in managing your expectations, and monitoring and tweaking your progress, can't really happen without the first. And this doesn't just apply to Facebook but to social audiences in general. Thankfully, the platforms themselves give us tools to help gather the information we need.

CROWDSOURCING

Besides tapping your own customers for ideas on what they're looking for, what are some other ways to use the power of the crowd to help you gather information and amplify your message? Surveys, polls, peer groups, and brand/consumer groups are just a few of the social tools available for harnessing the power of social media to gather information critical to your brand. Use crowdsourcing tools like these for both listening and disseminating information.

THE LISTENING STAGE

Twitter is a great tool for researching just about *any* topic, so it can be of great use to you when looking for sentiment from the Twitter crowd around a particular phrase.

Other social tools for monitoring and listening include social management applications like Tweetdeck or Hootsuite, which help sort and aggregate streams of conversation. Another is Crowdbooster, which also sorts influential followers and top sharers and suggests the best times for you to post updates that have the greatest chance of reaching your audience. As we write this, application developers are hatching even more tools to help us sift through the noise and gather meaningful information. It's very much an evolutionary process.

When you're looking for more detail than a tweet can provide or want to drill down into a specific topic, "Questions" on LinkedIn is a good way to gather feedback. The format gives people who want to answer your question plenty of room to expand on the topic and leave supporting links. Be sure to connect with those who leave answers so you can follow up and rate their answers at the end of the question time frame.

Customer surveys are great online as well as offline for getting even more granular and honing in on what customers are really looking for. However, keep in mind that most people are strapped for time these days. If you really want people to help you with a detailed survey, make it worth their while. Offer a nice coupon or other incentive in exchange for their time, and follow up. Google's Consumer Surveys and SurveyMonkey™ are good online tools for creating and sending surveys.

Whatever method you use, don't be discouraged if you get some negative feedback. It's human nature to not want to face negative news; however, don't be afraid to ask "why?" Use negative feedback as an opportunity to connect personally for a one-on-one chat to ask the person why they felt this way. Ask for their suggestions on how you could make their experience better. Keep in mind that critics can be incredibly valuable for feedback. You'll want to address their issues quickly because even your worst critics (when turned around) can become your most dynamic advocates.

THE INFORMATION DISSEMINATION STAGE

As good as social tools are at crowdsourcing information for your listening phase, they're even better for helping you disseminate information. Here are three options to consider:

1. Blogger Outreach: Identify influential bloggers in your space and tap into their collective reach for syndicating your story. Developing those relationships take time, but it's well invested.

2. Content Syndication: Take advantage of bookmarking sites like Digg, Reddit, Delicious, and Stumble

Upon to create a content syndication network that will distribute and expose your content across social networks. Also sites like Kathryn's Social Buzz Club network, Triberr, and List.ly that enable vast syndication.

3. Firestarters: Influential outside experts can be very helpful if they have large audiences in your niche. These are the kinds of people whose influence is so great that one word can ignite a firestorm of activity. Identify these people, and reach out with an offer to help them (without expecting reciprocity). If the chemistry is right, great things can happen.

Do you see how crowdsourcing can help you gather and disseminate information more effectively? At the end of the day, however, making it your policy to develop good relationships with your customers, vendors, and others is what will differentiate your brand from the rest. Make that your priority. Create conversations that matter with those who matter to you. Fulfill the promises you've made before making new promises, and strive to make every experience with your brand remarkable.

Good relationships naturally lead to people wanting to share their excitement about great products with their friends and the rest of their network. Good relationships— those built on trust, transparency, and honesty—create your brand advocates. Conversely, bad relationships (or nonexistent relationships) naturally lead to people to want to share their frustration about poor products on social sites, such as your Facebook wall or as a comment on your blog. But how should you react when you get a complaint?

REAL TRUMPS PERFECT
EVERY TIME

Earlier we talked about avoiding the advertising trap, which is one of the first bad habits companies tend to fall back on after they develop social profiles. But when the inevitable complaint pops up about your company, that's when another bad habit can arise—trying to whitewash your brand profiles. Below are two of the biggest relationship killers we've seen in online communications by brands:

1. Ignoring or deleting negative posts: When someone posts a complaint on your Facebook page or sends out a negative tweet, there are two reasons why you shouldn't try to hide it. Firstly, ignoring a customer who is complaining is a sure-fire way to amplify their frustration with your brand. Be quick about responding to them, avoid emotional responses, and view that interaction not as something to dread but as a way to better your relationship with that customer. Remember that conversation about your brand is going on all around you, even if you're not participating. Make sure to have "listening posts" like Google Alerts for negative comments around your brand so you can give them attention fast.

    Secondly, whitewashing your social profile to only include positive posts doesn't help you. When someone checks out your page, they'll very often look at your stream to see how you interact with people. If they see that someone complained, they'll want to know how soon you responded and if it looks like you resolved the issue.

TWO EXAMPLES OF BRANDS THAT "LISTEN"

1. Best Buy employs a force of three thousand to help with customer service issues on Twitter. Customers tweet questions to the @Twelpforce Twitter handle, where Best Buy employees trained to perform effective customer service under the brand's "healthy usage guidelines" answer their questions. These employees cover a wide range of knowledge sets to ensure that customers get prompt, effective responses to their problems.

❑   Eurail, a fifty-year-old train travel business, uses social media to interact with customers on a one-on-one basis every day. The brand focuses on Facebook and Twitter to connect with travelers and actively listens for pre-sales questions or a problem during a pre-planned trip. Eurail uses a dedicated team of travel professionals to handle the Facebook and Twitter accounts, allowing them to provide timely responses to every query, and is recognized as one of the most social media friendly and technologically savvy travel companies in the world.

2. Taking Followers Offline to Resolve Issues: In the same vein of deleting negative posts, if someone

has a problem and comes to your social presence to try to get it resolved, the worst thing you can do is shunt them off to a customer service contact with a "form letter" response. Too often we see, "Follow us so we can DM you," on Twitter, or a quick move to traditional customer service channels on Facebook. People have an innate need to be validated—and blowing them off is the fastest way to sour a customer relationship. Sometimes there are things that have to be resolved offline for legal issues, but the majority of complaints or requests for help should be addressed promptly and publicly in social channels. At the very least, if you *must* send them offline, do so in a friendly, personal manner. Address them by name, thank them for bringing the problem to your attention, and so on. Walk a mile in your customer's shoes—how do you feel when you're ignored or made to jump through hoops by a company you deal with?

Mistakes are Inevitable. It's how you react to them that counts!
If your customers think you messed up (whether *you* think you did or not), take responsibility for the problem *and* the solution.
That's how credibility is strengthened and relationships are built.

Once you and your team develop the skills to converse properly with your listeners, advocates, and others at every stage of building your brand, practice will make the process second nature to you. Now you can concentrate on building systems to help you nurture your new relationships.

CHAPTER FIVE

PERSISTENCE, PATIENCE, PURPOSE

Practice isn't the thing you do when you're good. It's the thing you do that makes you good.

—Malcolm Gladwell

You've heard that consistency is the key to achieving success, right? But what does that mean in terms of building productive online relationships? It means developing reliable systems for communicating on the channels you've chosen in order to effectively "scale" relationship building. This requires what we call "The 3 Ps" of persistence, patience, and purpose. When developing these systems, start with your main purpose (or goal) in mind, persistently apply strategies to meet those goals, and be patient—results may not be immediate, but they'll be well worth your efforts.

Two factors that have a direct influence on how well you achieve ROR are the type and frequency of your communications and how you build credibility with your audience. Let's take a look at how we can use systems to influence those factors.

CONSTANT COMMUNICATION

Scaling relationships across channels requires constant communication and monitoring for opportunities to connect—not just posting one-way messages and updates. Just as you've developed systems for listening and gathering information, you should also develop them for communicating via social across all aspects of your business that affect relationships, including these four areas:

- ❑ Legal
- ❑ Production
- ❑ Customer Service
- ❑ Marketing

We'll go through these one at a time with some examples that will hopefully make it clearer, but keep in mind that all your social communications should be *authentic*, *genuine*, *interesting*, and *responsive*. If your correspondence lacks any one of these characteristics, you're asking for trouble. Remember, in social communications, people expect the "real deal" from real people, not the corporate boilerplate they're used to getting from traditional channels. Make sure you hit those high notes for each of these four categories:

LEGAL

Every organization has different needs and legal issues that must be considered when disseminating company information, particularly if your company traditionally sends all outward-facing correspondence through your legal team (more on legal implications in chapter 6). However, keep in mind that fitting *every* response through your legal team in fear of how people "could" respond can slam the door shut on opportunities to relate to people. It can put a real damper on your relationship-building efforts if not applied correctly. So how can you overcome this within legal parameters?

Let's say your legal team needs a week to review your social editorial calendar before you can post. That means you'll need to make sure that everyone's on board, from content developers to programmers, for getting that content calendar filled out and sent through your legal department on time. It also means that your content developers will need an advance understanding of what can and cannot be said (including any customer service people who will have customer-facing social roles). Make sure you include enough time to train them so their calendars have a better chance of navigating legal without holdups.

PRODUCTION

Use social media to do your due diligence on your current and potential vendors and manufacturers. For example, you can ask a question on LinkedIn, reach out to Twitter connections, or put keywords in Twitter search to find out the information you need.

CUSTOMER SERVICE

We talked about customer service earlier, but this point bears repeating: make sure you have systems in place for seeking out customer service opportunities, and converse with those in your social channels to resolve issues publicly and quickly. These systems can include alerts such as Google Alerts, which can be set up around key phrases. Many social monitoring tools like Brand Monitor or Radian 6 can also be set up to seek out and list posts on various channels that could be customer service opportunities for response.

The main thing here is to avoid keeping customer service in a silo; it needs to be incorporated into your social channels. It's also important to screen those who will have social responsibility, making sure the right personalities are in place. Bring your friendliest customer service faces into your channels and have them help you design a comprehensive social service strategy that's consistent. Periodically monitor progress and how well your team resolves issues.

MARKETING

Increasingly, brand visibility on social channels requires as much thought as a traditional marketing plan. Granted, things are a bit more dynamics in social, but your core content needs a strategy. Using an editorial calendar for this type of planning is crucial, and it should be coordinated across all social channels, but keep it fluid.

When you're planning your editorial calendars, remember that seeking and developing true relationships requires a constant flow of communication, not sporadic updates. Think consistency here; develop a plan for posting frequency, and stick with it!

Also have a plan in place for using news or other trigger events as well as planned posts to keep things timely and interesting. To be as responsive as possible, your team needs to be actively monitoring social channels (at least up until midnight EST). Being immediately responsive to people who leave comments on your profiles (as opposed to a nine-to-five call center) is the first step in developing deeper relationships.

Remember, don't just show up and post updates. Your entire marketing strategy should make the shift from blast messaging large groups of people to thinking more in terms of reaching individuals. Social gives you that opportunity, so dig in and reach out for opportunities to have one-on-one conversations.

START WITH YOUR BLOG

Although we talk a lot about social media platforms in this book, it's important to mention that your company blog is an essential part of how you provide the kind of content your readers are looking for. So don't neglect it!

People are looking for the kind of information online that they feel will be most helpful to them, and a blog is the perfect vehicle for delivering short, timely, educational pieces that hit the spot with information seekers. Plus, blogs are search-engine friendly, so they are helpful in feeding the algorithms that keep company websites at the top of search engines.

However, since the focus of this book is on building relationships, there are a few more things to consider than just posting articles and working the SEO angle. Here are four places to concentrate:

1. User-Friendly Navigation: Keeping your blog easy to navigate with intuitive category labels will help people find the information they seek much faster. Here again, doing your research on what your customers are looking for is essential. Also, make it easy for readers to leave comments and share your posts on various channels.

2. Look for Holes in Your Competition: Take a look at your competition's blogs and websites. Are there content holes they've missed that you can take advantage of? Companies that consistently provide lots of in-depth content have a bigger chance of attracting people who are actively looking for information. It's not who has the biggest Yellow Pages AD that develops more relationships; it's he/she who disseminates the most helpful information.

3. Don't Close Your Comments: Don't close the door for people to leave comments on your blog; doing so leaves the impression that you only care about what you have to say and are not willing to be responsive to others.

4. Commenting on Other Blogs: Look for other blogs in your industry (but not direct competitors) that have a good amount of traffic and comments, and contribute a comment (or designate members of your team to do so), but *only* if you think you can add value to the conversation. Be careful *not* to

promote your company here; just add some insight, and do it on a regular basis. Make seeking out and commenting on other blogs a part of your team's weekly activities. The more you contribute to the conversation happening around you, the more you'll be seen as a thought-leader (and people will click on your link to check you out).

These are a few areas that can have the biggest impact on your blogging strategy as it relates to building relationships, but they are by no means the only places to concentrate. The overriding question to ask yourself when you're working on any aspect of your company blog is, "What's the best way for us to keep readers coming back and recommending us to their friends and associates?"

DEVELOP RELATIONSHIPS WITH OTHER BLOGGERS

Another way to think about building community with blogging is to create relationships with other bloggers. As CMO of e.l.f. Cosmetics (EyesLipsFace.com) from 2008-2010, Ted pioneered a program to develop and utilize blogger relationships to exponentially increase and sustain the e.l.f. brand visibility. This leveraged the energy, talent, and networks of those bloggers, which not only expanded the reach of the e.l.f. brand but provided the company with a unique approach toward not just beauty but also accessibility, interactivity, and consumer engagement. At that time, the jury was still out on the business value of social media; however, e.l.f.'s social presence helped shift the brand from a six-hundred-store Target holiday test into a nationwide inline Target brand. The success of this program confirmed for e.l.f. (and a few other previously skeptical businesses) that building relationships with bloggers is absolutely of value to the company.

In fact, that e.l.f. experience was the catalyst that helped form Ted's original ROR (Return on Relationship™) philosophy, which we continually see bearing fruit with other brands today. Remember that your blog (as well as blogs of others) can and should act as your information content hub that feeds your other social community platforms. Building social credibility with your audience starts by romancing them with useful, helpful content and then seeking ways to deepen your relationship with them with consistent social nurturing.

So now that you know more about the importance of using "The 3 Ps" in your content, how can you translate the concept to your social communications?

INVESTING IN "SOCIAL CREDIBILITY" INSURANCE

The relationships you build in social circles act as a kind of insurance policy. Whether you realize it or not, you're building "social cred" every day—and if you do it right, it can act as insurance that can pay off big time when you need it most.

Think of social credibility like the cash value of a whole life policy. By paying your "social premiums" of authenticity and transparency over time, you can bank quite a bit of advocacy and loyalty value that accrues with every payment. Developing that kind of brand advocacy can help you later on when you're launching a new product, have a PR crisis (such as a simple blunder or defective product), or in any number of scenarios where you'll need folks in your corner. However, like a whole-life policy, your social cred insurance won't accrue any cash value unless you pay your premiums!

JetBlue Airways is a big-brand example of how building social credibility early on can pay off. After developing a consistently high sentiment rating (79 percent) in social channels, consider what happened at JetBlue when an employee did something completely unexpected that didn't reflect well on the brand.

A highly publicized event occurred in August 2010 at John F. Kennedy International Airport in which a longtime flight attendant (after having an altercation with a disembarking passenger) spouted an expletive-rich tirade across the airline's PA system, grabbed a couple of beers, and used the emergency chute to leave a plane. The incident had social media analysts buzzing because JetBlue took its time in responding socially—waiting forty-eight hours before posting something about the incident on their blog. As it turned out, their short, tongue-in-cheek response to the incident was just what the doctor ordered, albeit a little late, as noted in a *New York Times* article, "JetBlue's Response to a Fed-Up Employee's Exit[11]":

> On Wednesday afternoon, the JetBlue blog BlueTales offered the company's initial official comments. A post that carried the headline "Sometimes the weird news is about us ..." did not

mention [the employee] by name; rather, it slyly asked, "Perhaps you heard a little story about one of our flight attendants?"

"While we can't discuss the details of what is an ongoing investigation," the post continued, "plenty of others have already formed opinions on the matter. Like, the entire Internet."

The post concluded with a reference to the 1999 movie *Office Space*, which mocks work life in corporate America, and a salute to JetBlue's "fantastic, awesome and professional in-flight crew members for delivering the JetBlue experience you've come to expect of us.

Subsequent analysis of social sentiment surrounding the incident turned mostly positive after JetBlue's post and reflected only a slight downturn (to 70 percent) from the brand's generally positive scores over the year.

JetBlue's social policy was consistently engaging before the incident, so their social credibility was high. Even though they took some time to gather all the facts before responding, their social credibility was buoyed by their positive response, resulting in a minor blip (rather than a steep plummet) in brand sentiment.

Another example of how a big brand was able to leverage positive sentiment in the face of crisis was Toyota after their massive recalls in 2011[12]. Toyota's customers are quite loyal (both on and offline), but when Toyota's social media team saw an increase in negative social media sentiment during the press firestorm surrounding the recalls, they realized they needed to mobilize their brand advocates. They did so with a story campaign on Facebook called Auto-Biography. Tapping their strong consumer advocate base, they asked owners to share their experiences on Toyota's Facebook page, from the "wonderful" to the "crazy" to the "not-so-happy." Tens of thousands of individual stories (overwhelmingly positive) were submitted, reaching hundreds of thousands of visitors. Many of the stories were about safety, and this outpouring of brand advocacy did a great job of countering the trending perception of Toyotas as unsafe.

So how can your brand build up this kind of credibility? As these two samples show, delivering consistently positive consumer experience is essential, both on and offline. Always think about adding value to the lives of your friends and followers whenever you interact in the social space, and give your social followers a voice. Communicate your value system to your social team, and make it a priority to always, always, *always* be thinking about helping, nurturing, and educating. Go out of your way to do it. Be proactive and creative in thinking up new ways to help your customers and prospects get what they need, and put your promotional stuff on the back burner.

Relationships Are Like Muscle Tissue ...

The more they're engaged, the stronger they become. The ability to build relationships and flex that emotional connection muscle is what makes social so valuable.

The bottom line is that by always being authentic and transparent in daily communications and consistent in delivering value, you can build the kind of credibility and trust that turns followers into brand evangelists. Not only will they buy things from you and tell their friends, they'll defend you and help you out when the need arises.

CHAPTER SIX

GET OVER YOURSELF

The greatest mistake you can make in life is to continually be afraid you will make one.

—Elbert Hubbard

In the last chapter we talk about the importance of "The 3 Ps" and how to develop social credibility and add value to your social communications. However, it's easy to fall back into bad habits, such as the advertising trap and whitewashing, if you're not careful. In fact, it takes a conscious effort not to do so. Why? In our experience, the main reason is fear. Although social has been around a few years, it's still a new concept for many brands to wrap their minds around.

We like roadmaps and blueprints—formulas that are tried and true. But for the first time in our collective memory as marketers, we can't control the conversation around our brands. The social phenomenon has thrown us for a loop, and that can be pretty frightening.

In fact, in a Harvard Review blog article entitled "Most Organizations Still Fear Social Media," authors Anthony Bradley and Mark McDonald reported that "most organizations...still view social media as a threat to productivity, intellectual capital, security, privacy, management authority, or regulatory compliance," according to their Social Media Readiness Assessment Survey[13].

As the Harvard Review article points out, fear causes companies to become either cautious toe-dippers or to shun social media:

> The trouble with a fearful attitude is that an organization often doesn't take a specific stance: it discourages and even prohibits the use of social media. While this approach reduces the potential for undesirable behavior—that's the reason for restriction—it also stifles any business value that might be derived from grassroots use of social media.

But if we let fear rule our actions, then we'll never move forward. Times have changed, and we need to let go of some of those fears or be left behind when the tide goes out.

GETTING OVER THE FEAR OF CRITICISM

Fear of criticism is perhaps one of the biggest stumbling blocks to social growth, and one of the first things we need to "get over" if we're to get anywhere in developing relationships. In chapter 4, we talked about the dangers of ignoring negative posts or removing them instead of dealing with them head-on. Below are some real brand examples of why this is so important.

A LESSON FROM CHAPSTICK®

Fearful reactions on social platforms can seriously impact your brand reputation, especially trying to "whitewash" your social profiles, which the brand ChapStick® found out the hard way.

In 2011, ChapStick posted an AD that some people found offensive. A blogger responded by writing about it in a blog, and posted a message on ChapStick's Facebook wall—which was deleted by ChapStick. Other people began objecting to the image—and ChapStick deleted their comments too. People kept commenting, and the brand kept deleting, trying to shove the whole mess under the rug, which just made it worse.

Eventually ChapStick deleted the offending AD and posted an apology on their wall, but the damage to their brand was done. It's a shame because it could have been avoided had the brand not made the following poor choices:

Poor Choice #1 Staying quiet
Poor Choice #2: Trying to whitewash their public space
Poor Choice #3: Trying to make the whole situation go
               away

ChapStick's controversial AD didn't need to start a firestorm of negative feedback and perception; if it had been handled differently, it could have been a powerful opportunity to strengthen and broaden the brand reputation:

Fix #1: Respond—"out loud"—as soon as the first customer speaks up.

When it comes to social media, silence is often louder than words. A quick Facebook post from ChapStick in response to the first customer complaint could have opened a conversation, providing a chance for ongoing interaction and the start of a mutually respectful relationship between brand and customer. Other Facebook fans (or Twitter followers) who read that exchange would also get a chance to build a positive opinion about ChapStick because of their willingness to listen to—and really *hear*—the customer feedback.

Fix #2: Be Authentic and transparent

What brand would you be more likely to do business with: one that encourages and engages in open, honest (authentic) conversation with customers/fans/followers, or one that filters their public persona to portray a squeaky-clean image?

The true display of transparency is having the courage to admit possible imperfections and respond to negative customer feedback—not to simply remove a realistic piece of the picture and then not admit to the action when confronted, as ChapStick did with the following statement: "We apologize that fans have felt like their posts are being deleted and while we never intend to pull anyone's comments off our wall, we do comply with Facebook guidelines ..."

Fix #3: Embrace criticism

Criticism is a great opportunity to show what your brand is really made of. Will you run from it or take it as a chance to learn more about what your brand's customers/fans/ followers *really* want and need from you?

ChapStick tried (eventually) to leverage the situation as a chance to state their appreciation of customer feedback with this statement: "We're aware of the discussion going on across social media, and we're listening. We love our fans and adore your passionate voice around ChapStick. However, the problem is that after someone has their comment deleted, the declaration of love and adoration no longer means much. You can say you're listening, but until you ask your customers/fans/followers clarifying questions and share your resulting action plan, words are just words."

Listen, ask, listen again, then act ... and do it all over again.

These kinds of mistakes are not easily preventable. They will happen again and again, whether by low-level employees helping to scale messaging and response or by C-level executives who think they can say what they want. They are part of the "new" media landscape that is only going to evolve and make more content available and presentable within seconds. Mistakes will be made, abuse will occur, and we will all survive. Put valuable training, methods, and rules in place to do your best before the fact…and crisis management and contingency plans for when they do happen. It is now all about transparency and authenticity. Be prepared.

WHY TRANSPARENCY AND AUTHENTICITY ARE ESSENTIAL

The above example illustrates how important authenticity and transparency can be in online conversations—especially when an unpredictable event rolls around. You can't control the social conversation surrounding an event, but you *can* influence it if you handle it properly, and that goes for negative comments as well.

However, it's also important for brands to understand that they need to take responsibility for faux pas they commit online. For instance, Chick-Fil-A's brand reputation took a hit in July of 2012 when President Dan Cathy publicly took sides in a highly politicized issue (gay marriage). Compounding the problem, it was discovered that a Chick-Fil-A employee actually created a fake Facebook profile in order to post comments defending the company. This cast suspicion on the company and further damaged the brand's credibility.

Was it worth the brand's social reputation to declare a stance on a politically charged issue? That's a matter of opinion. However, we feel it's best for brands to avoid highly controversial issues, especially since any public statement by brand executives will be put under a microscope by those with differing opinions.

Fear of criticism often plays into everyday conversations online, and not just around controversial issues. Even if you're very careful to steer clear of political footballs, you can't please everyone, so the occasional negative post is bound to crop up. The trick is learning how to plan properly so they don't throw you for a loop and become bigger problems.

DEVELOPING A DISASTER COMMUNICATION PLAN

To keep negative posts from mushrooming into PR blunders, a good system to put in place is to brainstorm a disaster plan for negative postings or those that need a specific customer service or legal response. That way your social team can maintain responsiveness and still operate within legal parameters.

For instance, during an initial onboarding meeting with one of Kathryn's clients, a major laundry brand, she asked what would happen if someone posted that their laundry detergent burned a hole in their clothes—or worse, they accused the brand of causing personal injury. That was something the company hadn't considered. Kathryn worked with the client to put in place a plan that took into account the innocuous complaint or question (e.g., The coupons won't print; What kinds of clothes can I use this on? etc.), all the way to the worst case—someone was injured. Here's how she did it:

- ❑ First she conducted a month-long listening campaign. This included more closely monitoring the social channels to determine what, if any, consistent complaints or questions arose.

- ❑ Next she compiled a document that included set responses to common questions and complaints. Both Twitter and Facebook responses were drafted—approximately twenty to thirty for each. That way the client's legal department could review and approve them, but customers would get a response more quickly and the responses did not look "canned."

- ❑ She also performed the same exercise for other types of posts, including compliments. This way all communications were covered and the client was able to engage more quickly.

- ❑ Kathryn's plan also included a list of which types of comments and questions needed to be routed to different departments. For example, if someone said that their product caused injury, those comments would be routed to the legal department for review and response. Other general comments were routed to client services or the requisite departments. Lastly, the team decided specifically who would be responsible for responding to issues. It was clear that if they did not have a plan in place or someone experienced to handle it, things could go bad quickly, so they drafted a social media policy for distribution to all departments.

Do you see how developing a system like this beforehand can help your social team react quickly and appropriately when negative posts arise rather than becoming defensive and wasting time? Just remember to keep those relationship doors open and positive when responding to people—and personalize those responses.

ARE YOU *REALLY* LISTENING?

While developing a disaster communication plan can be a good way to keep communications from faltering, it's also critical to read between the lines. If you're getting an inordinate amount of negative posts, are you really listening to your customers? Are there patterns that you're missing simply because you're not seeing the forest for the trees? Do attitudes need adjusting?

Sometimes we are so committed to our own brand experience that we have trouble actually hearing when our consumers are trying to ask us to change. In order to work around that (natural and understandable) resistance, we need to take a step back from our fierce attachment to what we believe makes our brand successful.

One of the biggest relationship killers both online and off is an arrogant attitude—namely, telling your consumers that they're incompetent. For instance, Zach Rosenberg, cofounder of the blog *8-Bit Dad*, hits the nail on the head when he said in a blog comment[14]:

> One of the relationship killers I've been seeing
> a lot is brands engaging incorrectly—namely,

publicly telling a consumer that they're wrong or have somehow used their product wrong. If you're addressing a customer in public—GREAT! But if you're addressing them in public and telling them that they're too dumb for your product somehow, then you're letting them and everyone else within earshot know that you think your customers are idiots.

For example…a customer frustratingly tweets something like "@Company's online stock check sucks!" The worst thing a brand can do is reply with something like "Well, it's not really representative of the store's stock. Did you call???"

This sort of brand interaction is toxic. An employee is so rah-rah about how great their retail establishment is that they've forgotten that customer experience is the reason why the technology exists…

Zach's absolutely right—and this reaction isn't limited to online relationships. We've all seen examples of terrible face-to-face customer service interaction or have been victims of it.

For instance, Kathryn had an experience with Westin Hotels, where she felt she was overcharged for Wi-Fi in her room. When she argued the policy with the hotel clerk at checkout, she was told it couldn't be changed. However, when she pulled out her cell phone and began to Tweet about the issue, the extra charge was quickly removed.

Thankfully, the Westin employee recognized the negative word-of-mouth potential of this incident and was able to turn the situation around by exercising flexibility, thus preserving a good future relationship with Kathryn (as well as those in line behind her).

The trouble with exercising inflexible customer service with people online is that the audience "within earshot" is much bigger, and so is the potential fallout for your brand. Besides coming up with the negative post-disaster plan we mentioned earlier, there are two other ways brands can avoid this issue online:

1. Carefully Screen Your Online Customer-Facing Representatives: If you're going to outsource your social customer service or assign it to someone in-house, make sure the assignee has the right personality for the job. They should be customer-friendly, naturally helpful, and sympathetic. This is generally *not* the job for your IT or development staff or a part-time intern. Just because they set up your profile doesn't mean they're good at dealing with people. Train them properly, and make sure they understand the ramifications of what they do.

2. Don't Add Customer Service to an Already Overloaded Individual: Stress is one of the biggest contributors to reactionary responses. Don't be tempted to add customer service to someone's plate when they already have a full-time job. It's hard to keep your game face on when you're pulled in too many directions, and this type of interaction requires focus and calm.

Another customer service blunder that kills relationships is when brands refuse to let their employees interact on social channels as people. Remember that people who spend time on social media like to spend time with people—not logos. If you have a team of employees handling your social responses, don't make them hide behind the brand logo when they interact with followers—give them a voice and a face. For years we've been hearing about how Ford does a great job of this with their spokesperson, Scott Monty (@ScottMonty), by allowing him to build his personal brand along with theirs. Scott interacts with followers as himself, not the Ford brand, which humanizes the brand and fosters good communication. Ford realized early on that being able to see the team members behind the company and interacting with them personally makes a big difference in fan loyalty. However, many brands still aren't paying attention.

When a company censors its employees and doesn't allow them to participate in social discussion surrounding the brand, it's usually because they're afraid of "what might happen if…" They're afraid their employees will spend too much time on social or say the wrong things. These issues can be resolved with a comprehensive social media policy so all employees know how and when they can and should interact. Remember, your employees should be some of your best advocates, and a natural extension of your "public face." Employee censorship on social channels just doesn't work. Your people are your company's personality, so let them shine for you. If you don't trust your employees, maybe you have the wrong employees or a business approach that will be difficult to sustain in today's hyper-connected world.

STRIKING A BALANCE BETWEEN TRADITIONAL AND SOCIAL CHANNELS

Getting out of our own way when it comes to social communications is one thing, but what about traditional channels? Are they still viable? Absolutely! With the ongoing emphasis on maximizing marketing campaigns by using social tools, we need to remember that consumers still exist—and often still operate in—the bricks and mortar world. Marketers/Brands must carefully blend both online and offline interactions to effectively communicate and build relationships.

There's a great television bank commercial that highlights this issue. In case you haven't seen it, it shows a couple approaching the roped-off entrance of a bank building, where they are stopped by a gatekeeper asking what they think they're doing. The couple replies that they want to go inside and speak to someone, and the gatekeeper laughs and says something like, "But that's what the Internet is for!"

Technology is definitely becoming more integrated with our daily activities, but in spite of all the hype you hear about social replacing everything, it has not replaced consumer's need for face-to-face interaction and bricks-and-mortar experience. The challenge then is for you to find the appropriate balance between online and offline channels for your specific consumers.

Chances are your consumers will use multiple channels and switch in and out of those channels several times through the purchase process. They might see a television AD that references a social media channel for those with a specific interest or need. They might then spend time using social media to build connections with other people who share that interest/need, including brand representatives (if you're wise enough to be there and open to the connection). From there, your consumers may take coupons, deals, or recommendations from brand advocates and purchase either online or at a physical location. Follow-up might go back online to social media as consumers share their purchase experience.

There are, of course, many different ways to leverage both online and offline tools and interactions, so how should marketers decide what combinations to use? We suggest you follow what Ted calls a "lose, gain, and give" process:

1. *Lose* Your Assumptions: You know what they say about assuming … (Hint: it includes the first three letters of the word). Don't assume that you know your consumers' preferences (remember, you are *not* your own customer). Assumptions quickly lead to marketers telling consumers what to do and even forcing them down a particular communication or action path—a sure way to lose the consumers you are hoping to attract.

2. *Gain* Understanding: Without your assumptions, you can now pay careful attention to your consumers to gain an understanding of what they really want and need. Ask them questions (social media is a great tool for this), listen to their answers, and then ask more questions for clarification. Not only will you gain understanding about your consumers, you will also gain trust—a key ingredient in consumer purchasing decisions. When you give them the chance, your consumers can help you find the right online/offline balance for them.

3. *Give* What They're Asking For: Action is the external proof of understanding. Consumers want to be heard and understood, and the way to prove that to them is to take their feedback and implement changes to your marketing campaigns, products, and services accordingly. Consumer-influenced action quickly builds brand advocates who are so delighted by their experience of your brand that they can't wait to tell their networks about it.

No matter what tools and tactics you choose, however, make sure your message and the consumer experience is consistent across all points of contact and interaction. What you promise online needs to be the same quality experience you actually give consumers offline, and vice versa. Your customers' worlds are becoming more and more integrated, and the purchase path they follow will be the one that meets them both online and off.

CHAPTER SEVEN

ADDING VALUE BACK INTO RELATIONSHIPS

Each friend represents a world in us, a world possibly not born until they arrive, and it is only by this meeting that a new world is born.

—Anais Nin

Facebook has done an amazing thing—they now own the word *friend*. The problem is that they have *devalued* the word while adding value to their brand. In today's digital age, the word *friend* means (more often than not) that you exchanged a keystroke with someone. When we're concentrating on developing relationships, however, we need to (in Ted's words) take back the word *friend* and add value to it.

This applies to all our social relationships online. Facebook, Twitter, LinkedIn, G+—basically all your connections—tend to become amorphous crowds over time, and we only truly interact with a precious few. We are missing the chance to use social media as a tool that facilitates real relationships because few of us actually take the time to connect in the ways that a real friend would.

So how do you change this? Start with breaking completely out of your online world for a moment and doing something really cutting edge: pick up the telephone and call someone! Ted likes to remind people when he speaks at conferences that the most prominent word in iPhone is *phone*. Make someone feel special by connecting voice to voice with them and having a real-time conversation.

So before you send off that next e-mail, start to text someone, or post an online message, take a moment to ask yourself if the relationship would be better served with a personal contact. If you want to add value to your relationships, resist the urge to take social shortcuts, and remember that:

Friends are not just an audience. Friendship is a two-way interaction loop. Ask questions, listen to and *hear* the answers, and ask more questions. It takes ongoing interaction to get a clear path through the digital noise out there!

A friend is not a number. Think about how many times you hear television ads that end with "to us, you are not just a number; you're a person!" Remember that each interaction involves a real person. Yes, Ted and Kathryn have over has over four thousand Facebook friends, but they also pay attention and respond to all comments and postings on their walls and photos. Does it take time? It sure does, but all real relationships take time, so expect nothing less!

A friend has shared interests. Friends connect around shared interests, which attract additional friendships that turn into communities of interest. *You* are the hub of your personal social media "community of interest," so consider it your responsibility to provide content relevant to your friends' interests. Hint: if you are authentic in your online and offline "profiles," what you are naturally inclined to share will automatically be of interest to your friends. Save yourself some effort and just be genuine from the beginning.

Friendships require maintenance. We are all calling these tools "social media," yet we are becoming *less* social. Facebook status updates do not count as a relationship. Back and forth conversation *about* your status update, however, is a much more social interaction. But don't let it end there. Take the initiative to reach out and give value rather than expecting everyone to come to you. True friendship requires an ongoing effort to contribute to the flow of giving and receiving.

Friends do unto others. The way you engage with people makes an impression no matter what tool you are using. Look at your own behaviors and ask yourself, "Would I want to be my friend?" Are you noticing and affirming the value of individuals and groups in your network? Are you genuinely interested and paying attention to the people behind the texts and words on a screen? Are you going out of your way to be of service to others in your network? What kind of friend do you want to have and to be? A real friend is not just a number and a photo on the screen.

Make a conscious effort to re-evaluate the word *friend* as you currently think of it the next time you're on social channels. Look at your own behaviors and ask yourself, "Would I want to be my friend?" Are you doing what it takes to be a "real" friend, or have most of your online relationships faded into the crowd?

CAN WE HAVE TRUE RELATIONSHIPS WITH MILLIONS?

Speaking of re-evaluating social friendships, it might be relatively easy to work on developing true relationships when your social crowd is relatively small, but what happens as your profiles grow? Can brands realistically expect to maintain relationships with an ever-growing number of followers, or does ROR suffer due to the time constraints of trying to interact with so many?

This is a conundrum for many growing brands, and social experts have been batting it back and forth for a while now. As our lists get bigger and bigger, should we talk with everybody who reaches out to us or concentrate on a few? Some scientists assert that we have the ability to maintain relationships with a maximum of around three hundred people and that everyone else falls by the wayside.

While that may be true, you have to make choices about how you interact with people socially based on what works for you and your audience. There's really no right and wrong here—unless you switch gears entirely and break your "brand promise" to your readership somewhere down the line.

Yes, there's only so much time to go around, but your audience understands that and appreciates the limited amount of time you can give them. You have to "walk the talk" of engagement, interaction, and relationship building or pay the price in brand reputation.

However, keep in mind that there may be followers who don't reach out to you directly, but they still watch the conversation and participate vicariously. So it's not just about whom you interact with and respond to individually. Those who see you interacting with others will feel a part of that interaction simply by observing and knowing you are having those conversations.

For any brand, the important thing to remember is to always be listening to your audience, responding to feedback, and doing the best you can with the time you have. So can you maintain meaningful relationships with thousands of people at a time? No, but every touch is important, no matter how small, and those relationships will scale when conducted in full view of everyone.

Think of it this way: individual touches are like relationship seeds. You have a much better likelihood of reaping a good harvest when you sow widely, but only if you prepare the ground with value and nurture with authenticity. How you do that is up to you; what's right for your brand may not be right for another with a different audience. There is no cookie-cutter approach that will produce the same results for everyone, but whether you're a one-man show or a company with an entire staff of socially facing employees, being true to your brand and genuine in your audience interactions will always bear more relationship fruit.

LOOK PEOPLE IN THE EYE DIGITALLY

When you meet people online, especially in a fast-moving stream like Twitter, what are some best practices for interaction? Well, think about social interaction the same way you think of meeting people face-to-face.

Isn't it annoying when you're trying to have a face-to-face conversation with someone and the other person is looking all around the room and not really "there" with you? That often happens at networking events and conferences where there's a lot going on around you in the room, but good networkers make a conscious effort to "look people in the eye" and actually focus on them during conversation. So how do you do that digitally? Here are some tips:

- ❑ Make it a point to actually look at their profiles. See if you have anything in common, and use that as part of your communication to make a personal connection.
- ❑ Always use their name when responding. Do this even if it takes a few extra steps to find it out, particularly on Twitter where lots of users have handles that are abbreviations, company names, or nicknames.
- ❑ Make sure you follow the conversation until its conclusion. You wouldn't walk away from a live conversation in the middle of it, would you?

Also keep in mind when you're interacting socially to follow the "unwritten rules of etiquette," and respect people's personal space. Nothing's more annoying to people than having a brand reach into their social space uninvited with a pitch. Earn the right to communicate what you have to offer, and do not make it all you do. How popular would you be if you went to a cocktail party where you didn't know anyone and immediately stood on a table and started shouting in a loud voice about what your company's got going on this week? If you value relationships, think of social media as a digital cocktail party and obey common-sense rules of etiquette.

IT'S A BALANCING ACT

Back in the forties and fifties (when people still took etiquette lessons), the art of developing relationships seemed more genteel—but things moved a bit slower then. Starting with the "me" generation of the sixties, we stopped teaching the social niceties—and that was a mistake. We need them now more than ever! Our need for personal touch and human interaction hasn't changed, but our ability to truly connect with others (at least for the last few generations) has been hampered.

In their best-selling book *Trust Agents*, authors Chris Brogan and Julien Smith talk about these concepts of getting back to basics as humans in order to engender trust in people. Things like asking about other people *first* (*How are you? What are you doing?*), understanding the culture (*listening*), promoting others twelve times more than you promote yourself, using a picture of yourself rather than a logo in social interactions—and others. And let's face it— relationships go nowhere without trust, so we need to sit up and pay attention.

It's almost as though we have to reach back to earlier generations to learn basic relationship concepts in order to be successful in the digital age. And that's tough because there's less personal time in our day. However, we have to find that balance. Technology has shoved us onto a track so fast that everything (and everyone) goes by in a blur. We can't stop the train and get off (as much as we'd like to), but we need to relearn how to slow down, work on developing trust-engendering relationships, and heck, just be nice to people.

Earlier we talked about getting out of your own way and practicing authenticity and transparency, all of which build trust and add value to your relationships. However, that kind of value can't be measured in dollars and cents. So how do you know when you've got it right? What's the magic formula? Next we'll explore ways to measure how you're doing.

CHAPTER EIGHT

HOW DO YOU MEASURE ROR?

Profit in business comes from repeat customers, customers that boast about your project or service, and that bring friends with them.

—W. Edwards Deming

What is one of the first things that come up when a new tool or process is introduced to a company? Metrics. What are the numbers we're aiming for? What will tell us if the implementation of a process or tool was a success? How will we get that information and make sense of it in a way that can inform our business strategy?

These questions—plus a few new ones—need to be asked as we begin taking social media integration seriously in our businesses and marketing strategies. But what does that mean in terms of building relationships?

Defining metrics around social media has been challenging, and early on many people said it simply could not be done. Now, however, we are learning that social media use and impact measurement *is* possible, but not by applying traditional metrics and methodologies. Granted, you can measure the ROI of social advertising campaigns just as you would any other type of advertising, using the simple formula:

$$\frac{\text{Benefits} - \text{Costs}}{\text{Costs}} = \text{ROI}$$

You can measure sales derived from specific links, how many people saw your ads or clicked through, etc. (because it's advertising, the traditional ROI formula works). In fact, any kind of social initiative that has some sort of tracking method (such as web tagging) can be measured—especially for retail brands. But trying to link income directly to the relationships built on a channel is a different story. When Eric Qualman (author of *Socialnomics*) was asked how to measure return on social media, he answered, "How do you measure the ROI of your phone?"

The mistake we see being made is that we're trying to measure social engagement with the same tools with which we measure every other digital touch point. E-mail, search, even banner ads, have spoiled marketers into thinking everything can be *and must be* measured with the same metrics used to gauge success in other mediums. That's simply not the case with social, which must be viewed as two mediums: communication as well as marketing. To measure the impact of social communication (and relationships in general), you have to take your advertising hat off and be willing to learn a new formula. So put that hat in the closet for a few minutes, and we'll walk you through a new way of connecting the dots.

SETTING CONDITIONS OF SATISFACTION FIRST

One of the most important new ways to establish social media metrics is to set "conditions of satisfaction" (a concept promoted by Jeffrey Hayzlett, former CMO of Kodak and author of the best-selling book, *The Mirror Test*). In other words, what are the specific outcomes that will bring satisfaction to you, your brand, your business, and your customers? Notice how the word *satisfaction* here requires you to think not just about actions but about the whole experience resulting from the outcomes. This is absolutely critical for successful social branding.

While Jeffrey applies this concept primarily to employees, vendor services, etc., it should also apply to your social efforts. Since social campaigns need to be built on relationships, setting up conditions of satisfaction should include words like *trust*, *engage*, *authentic conversation*, and *online reputation*—all things that are at the heart of a successful social presence.

Every organization will have different social conditions of satisfaction based on the company's specific and unique goals, vision, and values. This ensures that the information gathered can strategically inform your decision makers. Aligning your conditions of satisfaction with the heart of the company gives you the blueprint for planning engaging customer experiences with your brand. So don't take another step until your conditions of satisfaction are set.

MEASURE IN STAGES

Initially, as you're building your social media audiences and testing, there are three stages to measure:

- ❑ Audience growth
- ❑ Reactivity (getting them to take an action)
- ❑ Stickiness (keeping them coming back, engaged, and interacting)

Luckily, there are lots of applications that help marketers look deeper than just audience growth and get better insights on how they're doing with the other two stages, which is where "engagement" resides. While there is no one number that will give you the entire picture, most platforms will give you certain metrics on the reach of your posts and how many reactions (likes, comments, shares, etc.) they get. Keep in mind that the "stickiness" factor is influenced by how well you encourage back-and-forth conversation.

USE A BALANCED SCORECARD FOR A BIGGER PICTURE

Engagement is just one measure to track in social media (and it's an important one), but businesses need a broader picture of how social meets corporate objectives. Yes, executives want (and need) to see a financial return, but the answer doesn't lie in trying to quantify every aspect of your social presence. In fact, a recent Forrester Report, *The ROI of Social Marketing*[15], discusses the need to monitor outcomes rather than trying to attach financial measures to things like tweets, likes, followers, reviews, and comments. Basically, we need to monitor social's effects across four key business perspectives to come up with a balanced view (or scorecard):

- ❑ Financial
- ❑ Digital
- ❑ Brand
- ❑ Risk Management

Of course, we always need to track whether revenue increased or cost decreased over the period we're measuring, but the other three factors in the scorecard influence the financial picture, so we have to keep track of them too. How have we enhanced our digital assets, both *owned* (websites, blogs, communities) and *earned* (mentions in other channels)? Have consumer attitudes about our brand improved? Are we more prepared to respond to attacks or problems that affect our reputation? These are all important benefits that building social relationships can provide, so asking these questions (both when you're setting up your conditions of satisfaction and later as you're measuring progress) can help guide your steps.

The important thing to remember is not to develop too narrow a focus when measuring social initiatives. Social is still changing and maturing, and metrics will need to mature along with it. The platforms that are popular today may disappear tomorrow in favor of the next best tool, which will likely have a new set of metrics to learn.

We need to keep in mind that, going forward, long-term brand success will not be dependent on a specific social media tool (or a set of them); it will be relative to the depth and breadth of the relationships built (using the tools available) where the people find themselves communing. Building relationships and interacting with consumers is where the commerce of the future is heading. Yes, you can track ROI to a certain extent, but in the bigger picture, ROR looks something like this:

Social Media drives engagement
Engagement drives loyalty
Loyalty correlates directly to increased sales

ROR (#RonR) = ROI

CHAPTER NINE

CONCLUDING THOUGHTS

Neither a wise man nor a brave man lies down on the tracks of history to wait for the train of the future to run over him.

—Dwight D. Eisenhower

The world of business today is undergoing some major shifts, and change is always difficult and stressful. Just when we thought we had everything down, the social revolution came along and jerked the rug out from under us but created huge opportunities at the same time. Many of us resist change for as long as possible—that's just our nature. But you probably picked up this book because you know that you'll have to change, and soon. Social's global impact on how business is done has become an inescapable juggernaut; adapt or be left behind.

Does that mean you have to throw out everything you've learned about marketing since the invention of the telephone? Absolutely not. When large technological shifts happen, there are always things you can, and must, take with you. Don't ever forget your marketing lessons—those basic tenets still hold true. However, it's more important to learn to discard those things that don't serve you anymore.

In this book, we've shown you some ways to break out of some of those old habits and practices that not only don't serve your business but can actually do major damage to your brand and lower your competitiveness. Things like:

- ❑ Not listening to customers, or listening but not taking any action (which means you aren't really hearing)
- ❑ Not employing a "customer service" attitude in every aspect of business communication
- ❑ Not recognizing the importance of bridging the gap between customer service and marketing
- ❑ Censoring employees on social channels due to fear
- ❑ Using social as a broadcast medium rather than a two-way communication medium
- ❑ Attempting to control the social conversation instead of participating and guiding

We think it's interesting that in many ways unlearning these deadly habits requires relearning some basic principles of human psychology. It's almost as if we've forgotten how to play in the sandbox—to be curious and fun-loving, to be helpful to each other, even just to be nice to each other!

After all, the social revolution didn't come about to give businesses a bigger squawk box. It's all about reconnecting as individuals and sharing our experiences. It's about building human relationships one person at a time, but on a much broader scale than any of us imagined a decade ago.

Is it difficult to switch gears? Yes, but it's not impossible. Are there shortcuts to doing the work? No, and don't let anyone else tell you otherwise. However, doing the work forces you to re-examine how you interact with customers, vendors, employees, and each other and to attach value to the very act of developing those relationships and nurturing them. We hope we've made that a little clearer for you in these chapters.

We talked about the importance of courtship and humility and about the art of networking, crowdsourcing, and learning from your mistakes (and the mistakes of others). Brand advocacy, authenticity, transparency in business dealings—these and the other ideas put forward in this book aren't new; we're not teaching you something you didn't already instinctively know. However, the examples in this book show you how these fundamental concepts need to be reapplied to business today and why.

The things we valued and measured yesterday are already fading as technology moves us forward, but the power and value of relationships remains. No matter what new thing comes our way tomorrow, adapting to it with the core goal of relationship building will always serve us.

We hope a few light bulbs went off as you read this book and that you're already thinking of ways you can use what you've learned here to improve your business relationships. If so, then we accomplished what we set out to do. So don't keep it to yourself; pass it on to someone else who could benefit. You never know where that relationship will take you.

Relationships *are* the new currency. Honor them, invest in them, and start measuring your ROR.

ENDNOTES

1   Nielson. (2009, Jul 7). Global Advertising: Consumers Trust Real Friends and Virtual Strangers the Most [Web log message]. Retrieved from http://blog.nielsen.com/ nielsenwire/consumer/global-advertising-consumers-trust-real-friends-and-virtual-strangers-the-most/

2   Neff, J. (2011, Mar 8). Social Sampling Scores Big for Kleenex as a Million People Share Packs. *Adage.com.* Retrieved from http://adage.com/article/news/social-sampling-scores-big-kleenex/149272/

3   Mandese, J. (2012, Oct 3). NBC News Kills The Cemographic, Personafies its Viewers Instead. *mediapost.com.* Retrieved from http://www.mediapost.com/publications/article/184424/ nbc-news-kills-the-demographic-personifies-its-vi.html?ed ition=51949#ixzz28SXNlsO9

4   Facebook Traffic and Demographic Statistics. (2012, October) in *quantcast.com.* Retrieved from http://www. quantcast.com/facebook.com#!lifestyle

5   Youtube.com Traffic and Demographic Statistics (2012, October). in *quantcast.com.* Retrieved from https://www. quantcast.com/youtube.com#!lifestyle

6   Echo, S. (2012, Mar 28). 16 Very Interesting Pinterest Infographics. [Web log message]. Retrieved from http:// ibrandstudio.com/inspiration/pinterest-infographics

7   Twitter.com Traffic and Demographic Statistics. (2012, October) in *quantcast.com.* Retrieved from http://www. quantcast.com/twitter.com#!lifestyle

8   Walsh, M. (2012, Jan 23). Consumers View Social Marketing as Invasive. *mediapost.com*. Retrieved from http://www.mediapost.com/publications/article/166313/study-consumers-view-social-marketing-as-invasive.html

9   Sherman, E. (2012, Feb 28). Is Your Social Media Marketing a Turn off? *inc.com*. Retrieved from http://www.inc.com/erik-sherman/is-your-social-media-marketing-a-turn-off.html

10 Porterfield, A. (2011, Sep 26). 9 Facebook Marketing Strategies to Build Super Fans *socialmediaexaminer.com*. Retrieved from http://www.socialmediaexaminer.com/9-facebook-marketing-strategies-to-build-super-fans/

11 Elliott, S. (2010, Aug 11). JetBlue's Response to a Fed-Up Employe's Exit. *nytimes.com*. Retrieved from http://www.nytimes.com/2010/08/12/business/media/12adco.html?_r=0

12 Greenleigh, I. (2011, Feb 15) How Toyota and UPS use Social Media as Reputation Defense. [Web log message] Retrieved from http://www.bazaarvoice.com/blog/2011/02/15/how-toyota-and-ups-use-social-media-as-reputation-defense/

13 Bradley, A., McDonald, P. (2012, Jul 20) Most Organizations Still Fear Social Media. *Harvard Business Review* [Web log message]. Retrieved from http://blogs.hbr.org/cs/2012/07/most_organizations_still_fear.html

14 Rubin, T. (2012, May 9) Relationship Killers: Four of the WORST Mistakes Brands Make in Social Media. [Web log message]. Retrieved from http://www.tedrubin.com/relationship-killers-four-of-the-worst-mistakes-brands-make-in-social-media/

15 Elliott, N. (2012, Jun 20) The ROI of Social Marketing. *forrester.com*. Retrieved from *http://www.forrester.com/ The+ROI+Of+Social+Marketing/fulltext/-/ E-RES57009?objectid=RES57009*

ABOUT THE AUTHORS

TED RUBIN

Ted Rubin is a leading social marketing strategist and in March 2009 started using and evangelizing the term ROR, Return on Relationship™…a concept he believes is the cornerstone for building an engaged multi-million member database, many of whom are vocal advocates for the brand, like the one he built for e.l.f. Cosmetics (EyesLipsFace. com) as the Chief Marketing Officer between 2008 and 2010, and the one built for OpenSky where Ted, was the Chief Social Marketing Officer.

On May 1st, 2011 Ted announced leaving OpenSky and accepting the position of Chief Social Marketing Officer at Collective Bias (whose Advisory Board he joined in January 2011). Ted is also on the Advisory Boards of Blue Calypso, Chinoki, OpenSky, SheSpeaks, Zuberance, and Crowdsourcing Week.

Ted has a deep online background beginning in 1997 working with best selling author, entrepreneur and agent of change Seth Godin at Yoyodyne, which was acquired in Q4 1998 by Yahoo!

Many people in the social media world know Ted for his enthusiastic, energetic and undeniably personal connection to people. Ted is the most followed CMO on Twitter and has one of the deepest networks of any marketer in the social arena. ROR is the basis of his philosophy…It's All About Relationships!

Personal philosophy: "Life is not about waiting for the storm to pass… it's about learning to dance in the rain."

Connect with Ted… http://TedRubin.com or @TedRubin

KATHRYN ROSE

Kathryn Rose is an award-winning best-selling author, social media keynote speaker, and social media strategist and trainer with clients ranging from multi-million-dollar corporations to small business owners and entrepreneurs. She has a twenty-plus-year career in sales and marketing and has created successful communities for her clients totaling over 2.5 million fans, followers, and connections.

Prior to her career in social media marketing, Kathryn was a top Wall Street sales executive, responsible for over $100 million in sales per year. Her personal philosophy is "Success through Collaboration." She uses her unique relationship-building techniques to build a lucrative referral network.

A sought-after social media and relationship marketing speaker and trainer, Kathryn is also the CEO of the Social Buzz Club, the world's first online marketing collaboration network. She is the author of seven books on social media marketing: *The Step by Step Guides to Twitter*, *Facebook*, *SEO/Video Marketing*, and *LinkedIn for Business* and *The Parent's* and *Teens Guides to Facebook*, as well as the best-selling book *Solving the Social Media Puzzle: 7 Simple Steps to Planning a Social Media Marketing Strategy for Your Business*.

Kathryn has been featured on foxnews.com. msn.com, in television Good Day Philly, Channel 12 News, among others, and in major media outlets such as Woman's Day.

Kathryn resides in the Boston area with her husband, Howard; their two children, L.J. and Lorelei; and their dog, Mallomar.

Connect with Kathryn *http://katroseconsulting.com* @katKrose